Guided by the Voice of Spirit
A Journey of a Medium

Terri Tucker

Copyright©2019 by Terri Tucker
All Rights Reserved
For more information about permission to reproduce selections
from this book
Visit: chickswithspiritualgifts.com
ISBN: 9781707285570

DEDICATION

This book is dedicated to my sister Nikki Tucker.
Thank you for all your love, support, encouragement, and inspiration.
You are my best friend and partner in crime.
I wouldn't be on the journey without you!
I love you, Sponge!

"It is not the critic who counts; not the man who points out how the strong man stumbles, or where the doer of deeds could have done them better. The credit belongs to the man who is actually in the arena, whose face is marred by dust and sweat and blood; who strives valiantly; who errs, who comes short again and again, because there is no effort without error and shortcoming; but who does actually strive to do the deeds; who knows great enthusiasms, the great devotions; who spends himself in a worthy cause; who at the best knows in the end the triumph of high achievement, and who at the worst, if he fails, at least fails while daring greatly…"
Theodore Roosevelt

CONTENTS

ACKNOWLEDGEMENTS 11
FORWARD 13
PART I 15
CHAPTER 1- THE EARLY YEARS 17
CHAPTER 2- U OF A 31
CHAPTER 3- READINGS FROM LUPITA 39
CHAPTER 4- THE BALLPARK & JERRY 45
CHAPTER 5- THE FAN 59
CHAPTER 6- SPIRITUAL AWAKENING 69
PART II 83
CHAPTER 1- CLASSES, FRIENDS, & CHICKS WITH SPIRITUAL GIFTS 85
CHAPTER 2- CSG MY BUSINESS 101
CHAPTER 3- CSG A FULLTIME BUSINESS 119
APPENDIX 141
EVIDENTIAL MEDIUMSHIP 143
COMMON QUESTIONS 175
FINAL THOUGHTS ON RECEIVING A READING 177
AFTERWORD 179

ACKNOWLEDGEMENTS

I want to say thank you to the people that encouraged me, pushed me and have been on this journey of a Medium. You have been instrumental in my growth and development, but more importantly,
you are my tribe and my friends.

Kathy, Heather, Allison, Ann, Michael-Anne, Shannon, and Melissa: You all have been there from the beginning and continue to support me on this journey. Thank you for your friendship and love.

The Image Crew, McKale Girls, and Baseball Peeps:
Thank you for being my family.

The Girls from Harmony and Circle—Lorina, Jody, Christina, Jakki, the Karen's, Kim, and Corinne: You all have been my rock, confidants, and sisters. Thank you for all your love, support, and friendships.
You are my tribe and coven.

To Nancy, Zack, Tina, Bobbi, Patsy, and Joy:
Thank you for your friendships, love, and support.

To all my students and tribe members: I wouldn't be here without all of you! I realized the love of teaching from you! Thank you for allowing me to teach and build this amazing community and tribe that we have.

To all my clients: I want to thank you for entrusting me to give you readings or healings. It is such an honor, and I am so grateful.

To my cousin Alex: Thank you for the beautiful illustrations in this book; you are an Angel!

To Steve, AP, Jerry, Uncle Nick, and Grandpa: Thanks for helping me on my path as a Medium. I know that you are there supporting me all the way.

To my Spirit Guide, Teddy; Mediumship Guides; Mother Mary; Angels; Archangels; and my Spiritual Counsel: I would not be on this journey without you as my team. Thank you for trusting and guiding me along this spiritual path.

Lastly, thank you God, Source, One, Spirit. You have enlightened me, nudged me and helped me on this spiritual path. Without you I would be nothing. Thank you for allowing me to serve others on this journey as a Medium and to be continually *Guided by the Voice of Spirit*.

FORWARD

As a child, my life was different than most. Some might say my childhood was a training ground. You see, a female ghost lived in my house. My sister and I could see her. Even though we shared the same experience it frightened me. Somehow, I adapted; it was the only way I could survive. I could also feel other people's energy, see things of the paranormal, and just knew things that I couldn't explain. It was like second nature. I trusted it, but I wasn't sure why.

These abilities–you might call them intuition, a gut feeling, or something else–were my psychic senses. I didn't know that at that time, though; all I knew was that I could tap into an energy that other people weren't aware of or didn't possess themselves. That all changed when I was 17 and I left for college. That was when I left the paranormal in the past.

But Spirit has a way of getting you back on your road without you knowing it. At 25, I awakened. I became fascinated with the paranormal, metaphysics, and the unexplainable. I loved watching T.V. shows about Mediums, people who communicate with Loved Ones that have passed. I always thought that their abilities were amazing. Who knew that I had the ability too!

But it took me some time to recognize that ability. Spirit kept nudging me. When I started to pay attention, I slowly ventured down the path to discover my abilities. After a few years, when I finally opened myself up and trusted my childhood abilities, I became aware of an energy around me. Once this transpired, a wall inside came crashing down and I started to "hear" the Voice of Spirit. At first, I thought I was making things up and it was just in my mind. But I started to understand that that was not the case. More and more things kept occurring, and it became harder to deny. I finally realized that these were not just coincidences.

Once I finally took a leap of faith and trusted where I was being led, my life turned upside down. The world that I once knew seemed completely different, and I could see things clearer. Sometimes your foundation needs to be shaken up so you can rebuild something new. As I started to trust the experiences, synchronicities, and "knowings," I started to understand my journey. I was "awakened" to know that my path was spiritual.

Everyone comes to Earth with a purpose, and Spirit led me to mine. I was here to help, heal, and teach others on their journeys. My life purpose was to become a Medium. I didn't seek to become a Medium, but that is what I signed up for in this lifetime. When I realized this, my life started to change in ways that I never dreamed of.

This is my story on how that journey unfolded. I've had many trials and tribulations along this road, but I have encountered some amazing people too. Due to privacy, I changed the names of some people and clients, but the story is the same. This is how I was *Guided by the Voice of Spirit* to begin my journey of becoming a Medium.

PART I

CHAPTER 1- THE EARLY YEARS

Growing up, I always felt that I was different. I never seemed to fit in with the other kids. Because I felt different, I avoided playing with the kids at school. I would procrastinate when it was time for recess so I wouldn't have to play with anyone. Also, I lived in Wisconsin where it was cold most of the year. I didn't like the cold. This was another reason I wanted to stay inside too.

One time when I was around 7 years old, I found myself sitting alone on the playground at lunchtime. I was crying and asking God why I didn't have any friends. I told God I didn't like being here and wished I could leave. As I was having this conversation, my younger sister Nikki walked over and sat next to me. She noticed I was crying and asked me why I was so sad. I told her I didn't have any friends to play with. I cried more. Nikki told that she was my friend and would play with me. We got up and started to play. At that moment I felt happy because I was not alone.

Nikki was not only my sister; she was my best friend. She's was the only one who really understood me. She was the only one I could count on. That day I really needed her, and she knew it. It was a nudge from Spirit.

That was not the only time Nikki was there for me. Nikki had saved my life two years prior. I was swinging on a huge rope that our dad attached to our swing set. The rope somehow wrapped around my throat. I was being strangled. At that moment Nikki, who was 4 years old, felt an urge to walk the dog. Somehow, she was able to get the dog out of his cage and started to walk him. She could have turned right and not seen me, but she walked left and saw me dangling from the rope.

Nikki yelled for my parents, but they didn't hear her. Immediately she thought to get her red trike. Nikki wheeled the small bike over to me and told me to stand on it. At that point I managed to get the rope off my neck. I was coughing and coughing, trying to take a deep breath. I knew in my gut, that I had almost died. Once I had caught my breath Nikki told me that I was turning purple when she saw me. The rope also left a deep red burn around my neck.

When I asked Nikki how she knew to get her trike to help me, she said that the idea just popped into her head! Then, when I asked her why she was walking the dog, she said the same thing. The idea just popped into her head! Nikki never walked the dog before or after this. It was another nudge from Spirit.

I told my mom what had happened, and she yelled at my dad to take the rope down. My dad, however, didn't think it was a big deal. He finally took the rope down a few weeks later. Despite the huge rope burn around my neck, the incident was brushed off. It was at that moment I knew then that I had to take care of myself. This was also evident in two other instances where I almost died as well.

A year before the rope incident, for some reason, I decided to eat my aunt's paint set. I guess the paints looked tasty to a 4-year old! Well, the paints made me sick. My parents didn't want to take me to the hospital. Rather, my aunt had to talk them into it. I remember going to the hospital and eating charcoal to purge the paints up. At that time lead was in paints, but the ramifications of it was unknown. The doctor told my parents that it was a good thing that they brought me to the hospital because the paints could have poisoned me.

Once we got home from the hospital my parents let me know they were very upset with me. They yelled about the cost of the hospital visit. I remembered my father spanking me and putting me in time out. I told myself that I had to be a good girl and never go to the hospital again. However, the hospital topic came up again three years later.

When I was 7 years old, my father hit me in my nose with a horseshoe. He was drinking Old Style beer when the accident took place. Right before this happened, he warned me and my sisters to stay away from him because he was getting ready to play horseshoes. This was something that he always did. My sisters were on one side of him, and I was on the other. Right after he gave us this warning, I did what he asked and moved away from him. Under the influence of alcohol, he forgot that I was on the other side of him. As I went to walk around him, he pulled his hand in the backward position to throw the horseshoe. He hit me in my face, and I was knocked out cold for hours. I remember waking up on the couch later that night.

When I awoke, my parents were arguing about going to the hospital. Of course, they didn't take me. I am sure this was because of money issues and my father's drunken state. Instead, I laid on the couch with icepacks on my face the entire night. I didn't attend school for over a week. The incident was never discussed. After the incident, I had trouble breathing out of nose. I told my parents about it, but they brushed it off. Breathing out of my mouth became my new normal. These events may sound bad, but they are nothing compared to what transpired daily in my house.

To say that the environment of my house was intense would be an understatement. My father was always a controlling man, but it was worse when he drank. He was an abusive alcoholic. If he wasn't beating my mother, he was beating us kids. He would hit us with belts, sticks, fists, and steel boots. He used knives to threaten and control us. My father instilled fear into all of us. Everyone constantly walked on eggshells.

Now on the other hand, my mother was passive. I don't know if it was because she would get beat if she stepped in stop him. Or maybe she believed the abuse would eventually stop. Whatever the reason, I believe that my mom gave her power to my dad. It became easier for her to look the other way. As a child I couldn't understand why this abuse was happening. There were people in my mother's life who could have helped her out of this situation. But the abuse was well known among family and friend and yet nothing was done about it.

My parents were very religious, and we grew up in the Lutheran church. Missing a church service was not an option, let alone Sunday school classes each week. We were taught the 10 commandments, and my parents made sure we knew them by heart. One of the commandments is honor thy father and mother. Because of this commandment, I couldn't ask my mother why our father would hurt us. This would have been disrespectful in her eyes because children didn't have the right to question their parents. So, his behavior continued, and my mother didn't admit it or talk about it.

Turns out my mother had abilities (psychic senses) but didn't talk about it. I believe that tapping into the paranormal was one way my mother coped with the ongoing abuse. When my father wasn't home, my mother loved to work with the paranormal. She would have séances with her family and friends on Friday or Saturday nights. They would use her Ouija board and conduct table tipping in our house. Table tipping is used in séances. During the practice, people sit around a small table and place a finger or hand on it. Each question that is asked invokes paranormal experiences from spirits and to get the table to move, with the answer. They'd also give readings using my mother's tarot deck.

I saw so many strange things happen in our house during these occasions. During one séance that my mother conducted, she asked a question regarding her stepfather, Rollie. She wanted to know if he was a good person. At that moment, the table lifted a few feet off the ground and slammed back down on the floor. Everyone was stunned and didn't know what to do. We all knew that the question was answered correctly because Rollie was not a nice man. That was the final séance that night. And no one ever asked about him again! In other instances, I remember objects flying across the room or the lights going on and off. This was typical on most nights.

The many séances conducted over the years brought negative entities into our house. My mother never properly learned how to protect herself, others, or the environment. Unfortunately, it affected everyone in the house. However, it affected me the most. My abilities made being a child in this type of environment excruciating.

One my abilities is clairsentience (clear feeling), which makes me an empath. I am also a Medium (being able to communicate with people who have passed). At that time, I had no idea that I had abilities or was a Medium. What I did know was that I didn't want to be in that house around my father or other people. I was very sensitive to all these energies, and it caused me to become a very sick child.

Sickness caused me to miss half of my kindergarten year. I found out many years later that I almost didn't pass because of it. I wasn't just physically sick, but also emotionally and mentally drained too. I couldn't rest because of the negative energies in the house. The energies were most active at night when I tried to sleep.

I would see ghosts at night. The first ghost incident occurred when I was around 4 years old, but I didn't know it was a ghost. I just remember seeing a lady in the bedroom I shared with Nikki and my older sister Michelle. Nikki and I had bunkbeds across the closet while Michelle had a bed, right next to it. Michelle was not bothered by the lady ghost, but Nikki and I could see her. She appeared out of the closet with a flowy white dress and had long hair. She walked back and forth and would sometimes close our bedroom door. The lady never talked to us; she would just walk in and out of our room.

One day, I asked my mother why she was in our bedroom with a white dress on. She looked at me, told me she wasn't in our bedroom and that I must have been dreaming. She walked away and refused to hear any more about it. Right after this conversation, though, my mother went out and bought us a lamp. The lamp was to be used as a nightlight so we could sleep. If she heard us talking about the lady ghost, she placed a brighter watt light bulb in our nightlight! I am not sure why she thought this would help, but in her mind, she felt that it did.

As I grew older my mother finally acknowledged that she could see the lady ghost in our house. She told us that her name was Rose. Rose had died in the house years before my parents moved in. She would walk around the house, close doors, pull blankets off beds, and watch over us. Rose constantly walked into my parent's bedroom and pulled the blanket off their bed. My father always yelled at my mother for it. He didn't believe in the paranormal, but that changed one night when Rose awakened him by touching his feet. He told us that he woke up to a chill of cold air and saw her at the foot of his bed. That was the only time he spoke of her. Even though Rose was not a negative ghost, I believe that she was there to protect us at night from all the negative entities that roamed the house.

After many séances and strange occurrences that happened in our house, my father became more abusive. I believe this was why my mother stopped using any paranormal items, like the Ouija. She acknowledged that there were negative energies in the house. She also acknowledged that there were negative energies attached to my father too. He was drinking more and becoming more controlling and abusive. My mother felt that if she left the paranormal alone things would become better.

On the contrary, that thought was just an illusion. Her actions caused things to become worse.

One night my mother decided that she was going to burn the Ouija board and planchette. A planchette is a small board on casters that is used to spell out letters on a Ouija board. My sister Michelle and I walked with my mother to the basement. There we had a black wood-burning stove that heated the house in the winter. My mother went to the stove and threw some more logs into the fire. Then she threw the Ouija board and planchette into the fire. It was blazing hot when she threw it in, and she used the poker to push it into the flames. My mother closed the door to the stove, and we all went back upstairs to bed.

When my sisters and I woke the next morning, we noticed that my mother was in tears. We asked her why she was crying. She said she would show us, but we had to go into the basement. We all looked at each other and then followed her down the steps. As we walked down the stairs, I knew it had to do with the wood-burning stove. My mother opened the stove to show us that the Ouija board and planchette never burned! This didn't make sense because the fire had been blazing hot with several logs in there. We were all stunned and didn't know what to say.

My mother became hysterical. She just kept saying, "I knew that this board was evil." She immediately went upstairs to throw her tarot cards in the trash. Then she found the table for table tipping and threw that away too. She was in a frenzy. My mother looked at me and my sisters and said to never to discuss this incident. That was that. I don't know if my father knew what happened, but I do know that my sisters and I never spoke a word about it.

As I reflect, I wish my mother knew how to dispose of a Ouija board. Burning them is never an option. If you burn a Ouija board, the energies that are in the board are released into your environment. To properly dispose of a Ouija board, you need to bury it or throw it in the trash to be buried in a landfill. My mother felt she was getting rid of the problem unfortunately it was the worst thing that she could have done.

After the Ouija Board incident, I remember feeling extremely heavy and negative energy in the house. I knew I didn't want to be in the house, but there was nothing I could do about it. I was only 8 years old. Nikki could feel the energy too, and we both knew that we were not alone.

This became evident one morning when I was making peanut butter and jelly sandwiches. My sisters got ready while I was made our lunches for school. I retrieved the bread from the bread container and set it on the counter. As soon as I set it down, the bread loaf slid across the 3-foot-long counter. I was stunned. I picked the loaf back up, and it happened again.

At that point Nikki walked into the kitchen. I told her to watch. I picked up the bread loaf and set it back down. It slid across the counter again. I picked up the loaf took out a few slices and then put it in the bread container and closed the door. As I walked away, the bread loaf popped out of the container, flew across the kitchen and fell to the floor. Nikki and I just looked at each other not knowing what to do. I finally picked up the loaf of bread and left it on the table. Then Nikki and I ran out of the house because we knew it was the negative entities. This was the typical kind of activity that was occurring daily in our house.

Not only did we have prankster ghosts in our house, but other strange phenomena began to happen. Lights would turn on and off by themselves. I saw shadow figures creeping around doors and windows. I felt cold spots and negative energy in different areas in the house. I always had a feeling that someone was watching me, and I never wanted to be alone. Things would fall off shelves when no one was around. Items in our house were moved or put in places that they didn't belong. Doors would open and close by themselves. We also had several parakeets that died for no apparent reason. The list goes on and on.

Strange things happened everywhere in the house, but the worst of the negative energies resided in the basement. It was a typical cold, dark and dingy basement. But it wasn't the appearance that affected me, the "feeling" that I got when I was down there was the worst. It felt like a dungeon to me I couldn't breathe down there because the air was so heavy. I also felt eyes watching me. This was evident with the replica Mona Lisa painting that hung on one wall. You could literally see her eyes moving, like she was watching you. I have seen the real Mona Lisa painting at the Louvre Museum in France, and that one didn't scare me. Ours was creepy and different. I never wanted to look at it!

I tried my best to avoid the basement at all costs. But in the summers, my sisters and I sold worms for fishermen to buy. We stored the worms in the basement to keep them cool. I had to go down the basement numerous times daily, to collect the worms. I was grateful when summer ended because the worm business closed for the season. This meant that I didn't have to go down there as often. Ultimately, the basement was the worse room for entities because the Ouija board had been burned down there. Even to this day I still find that basement one of the scariest places that I have encountered.

I grew more afraid as the activity increased. I have few memories after the Ouija board because I was so traumatized. The incidents in the house scared me throughout the day, and sleep was no escape. Sleep was terrifying. Terrible nightmares caused restless sleep. I was profoundly clairvoyant (clear seeing) and would to see things physically or in my dreams that frightened me. I had the same reoccurring dream night after night. People chased me, and I tried to run away. But I would eventually fall. I hated that falling feeling, and I never wanted to fall in my dream. I didn't know what to do about this dream. My mother wouldn't listen, so I felt alone and frightened. The only thing I could do was pray to God to help me.

I remember crying and telling God that I didn't want to "see any more bad stuff" in my house or dreams. It must have worked. After my plea I didn't see the female ghost again or remember my dreams.

I didn't realize this as a child, but I learned later on that what you ask for is what you receive. It is the Law of Attraction. I asked not to be clairvoyant, and thus it was given. My clairvoyance was taken away, but my clairaudience (clear hearing) and clairsentience (clear feeling) became heightened. So, I didn't escape these abilities. One was taken away, but the other two abilities increased!

I wish that I still had my clairvoyance. Over the years I have asked Spirit to bring it back, but with little luck. I can see a bit of color out of my third eye, but it is still hard for me to dream. Whatever I asked for that night, has been hard to reverse.

I do know now that when I dreamt as a child, I was astral traveling to the Other Side. Astral traveling is an out of your body experience (OBE). The "falling feeling" I experienced was my soul falling back into my physical body. This is the feeling that you have when you are startled awake.

And who were the people chasing me? Well, those were my guides and angels! They were trying to help me, but in my child's mind I felt they were chasing me. I wish I knew all this back then because I would have been able to go to sleep at night!

The increased negative energies in the house contributed to my parent's marriage falling apart fast. My father became even worse than he was, and I tried to avoid him at all costs. He started to drink more excessively, which led my mother to lock him out of the house. Not to mention that he went to jail a few times too due to the alcohol. His behavior and demeanor were awful, and he was abusive daily. The house was a very toxic environment to say the least.

But, a glimmer of hope arrived. My parents announced that they wanted to move to Phoenix, Arizona. Our maternal grandmother, who we had never met, lived there. She was having problems with her eyes and needed help. When they told us of this news, I was so excited. I couldn't wait to leave this house and the state! I finally felt that I was going to be living in a safe environment. That turned out to be wishful thinking. We moved to Phoenix when the school year ended. I was 10 years old. The move changed nothing. My father's behavior was just the same.

My parent's marriage lasted about a year before they got a divorce. The divorce was the best thing that could have happened for all of us. We were free of living with my father's negative behavior and energies. We could finally breathe again! After the divorce, I didn't often see or speak to my father. I last saw him when I was 14 years old. After that, the only contact I had with him was when I sent him a letter. I told him how I felt about his behavior, words and actions. That was that. I was finally free of him and that chapter was officially closed!

Living in Phoenix, I loved the weather, people, and culture. I finally felt like I was at home however I didn't fit in here either at school. I was still a loner. I think this was because I was so shy and didn't trust people due to my father's abuse. I had a few friends, but I didn't really hang out with them. I focused on getting good grades and worked a few jobs to save money for college. I also stayed clear of anything that had to do with Ouija boards, tarot cards, or anything of that nature. I didn't want to be involved with the "dark arts" as I liked to call it. It would take me many years before I took part in anything of that nature again.

When I was 15, I met Steve and Carrie. They hired me to babysit their boys. The more I got to know the family, the more I became a part of it. Steve and Carrie supported and encouraged me. Ultimately, they are the reason I went to college. Steve became my mentor and acted as a father figure toward me. Carrie confided in me that Steve had always wanted a girl. I became like a daughter to him. This was another nudge from Spirit.

After watching the boys for some time, I learned more about Steve and Carrie. They met at the University of Arizona (U of A) in Tucson. College life was a part of their identities. Steve was a huge U of A fan and everyone knew it. They attended many games and events.

One day, Steve asked me where I was going to college. Truthfully, at that time, I didn't know if I would attend college. My mother never talked to us about college probably because we were extremely poor. But I didn't want him to know this. I told him I was thinking about attending a junior college. I had received a partial scholarship to a junior college, but I wasn't really thinking of attending.

Steve looked at me and told me that I was smart enough to attend a four-year university. He said that I could apply for grants and loans to pay for it and not to worry. At that moment Steve became a dad to me. He told me that the entire family was going to take me to Tucson to visit the U of A for homecoming in a few weeks. I knew in that moment that I didn't have a say in this matter and agreed to go.

One Saturday morning a few weeks later, the family and I drove to Tucson. I had never been to a college campus and was amazed by campus life. I remember walking around campus and feeling like I was at home. Carrie took me to see the different dorms and sites around campus. Later, we tailgated with their college friends. Everyone shared their college stories from U of A with so much love and joy. As we headed off to see the football game, it all seemed to be surreal. During the game I knew in my gut that I was going to attend this college no matter what I had to do. It was a nudge from Spirit.

After visiting the U of A, Steve advised me to look at other colleges too. He wanted me to be 100% sure that I wanted to attend there. I heeded his advice and looked at other colleges. I thought about Florida State and University of Hawaii because of the warm weather. But I decided they were too far from Arizona.

I did visit Arizona State University's (ASU) campus. ASU is U of A's rival. Steve was not a fan of the school. Nevertheless, I took a tour by myself to see if I liked this college campus better. As soon as the tour started, I knew instantly that this was not the place for me. It didn't have the same college campus feel that the U of A did. Again, I knew in my gut that the U of A was the place for me.

A week after touring ASU, I shared my feelings with Steve and Carrie. They were thrilled that I chose U of A. Carrie immediately helped me prepare for college. She gave me insight on what I needed to do to apply for college, like filling out loan applications, preparing for tests, and finding a dorm. It was a lot of work, but I made sure it was taken care of.

I was excited because I would be the first one in my family to attend college. My mother didn't want to take any part helping me apply to college, and that was alright with me. Then I encountered a problem where I needed her help.

I was only 16, and I needed her to sign the student aid forms. I literally had to beg her to sign her name on the forms. It took several weeks, but she finally agreed. I didn't understand why she didn't want to sign them to begin with! Rather I had to just let it go because it made me sad to think about it. A few weeks later I discovered the real reason on why her behavior was the way it was.

One day, my mother informed me that I needed to help her pay for things in the house. She started taking money out of my bank account, behind my back. Unfortunately, there was nothing I could do about it because I was under 18. The only thing I could do was stop cashing my babysitting checks. I was saving every penny for college, and I didn't want her to take anymore.

As before, Spirit stepped in to help solve the problem.

A month later, Carrie asked me why I was not cashing the checks that she wrote to me. I knew I had to come clean. I told her that my mom was taking money from my bank account, so I stopped depositing them. I was only 16, and I couldn't apply to get my own account. She just looked at me and didn't know what to say. Then she said that she would figure something out.

Carrie told Steve what was happening. He was stunned too. Steve decided that Carrie would open a bank account for me, and she would be the legal guardian on the account. Carrie took me to the bank the next day.

She opened an account for me, and I deposited all my checks from babysitting. I was so relieved. I never told my mom about this bank account. But she knew something happened because she told me that she wasn't going to buy anything for me. From that point on, I bought my own food, hair products, clothes, etc. I was on my own.

Soon after that event, it was time to take the American College Test (ACT). I had studied for this test, but I was not the best test taker. I was very stressed during the entire testing process. I felt that I needed more time with the questions, especially the math questions. After I finished the test, I just hoped and prayed that I had passed.

It took several weeks to receive the results. When I finally received them, I was devastated. I had scored a 12 on the test. The median score is 20. Once I found this out, I went to see my school advisor. She was not encouraging. She told me that I would not be a good fit for college. I left her office with tears in my eyes. I knew in my gut that I was smart enough to go to college.

I didn't share what I was told from her with anyone. I just asked Spirit to help me get into the U of A. A few months went by, and I finally received a package in the mail from the U of A. I was accepted! I discovered that my high school grades trumped the low ACT score. I was overjoyed and could not wait to share this news with Steve and Carrie. I took the letter with me when I went to babysit for them later that day. I was so excited to show them that I got in. They were happy for me and proud that I made it all happen.

I was also excited to show my mother the letter. Her reaction was the opposite of Carrie and Steve's when I shared my news with her. My mother told me that I was not smart enough and that I would fail out of college. She said that if I attended college that I was not welcomed back home. For most people this would crush them but for me it propelled me. This made me want to attend college even more!

I told Carrie about this, and she was stunned. She told Steve. He called me and told me that I could do this. When I hung up the phone, I knew that I needed to walk away from my mother too! It was another nudge from Spirit.

A few days before I left for college, Steve took me out to dinner at a fish restaurant. He shared his advice and insight on how college worked. He told me that if I needed anything to make sure I called them. He also told me that the entire family would be visiting soon because football season was around the corner. I just smiled and had tears streaming down my face. I felt so blessed because I felt I supported and knew that I was not alone.

College day arrived, and my mother's friend drove us to Tucson. I had never met her before. I don't remember why my mother decided to go with me. I just remember my bike on top of a station wagon packed with a few boxes of my clothes and things. It was a quick trip. We arrived and I took the few boxes to my dorm. I gave my mother a hug and that was it. As I walked into my dorm, I knew I was not going to look back.

Since that day over 20 years ago, I have only seen my mother for a few family occasions, like when Nikki wed and had a baby. Nikki maintained a relationship with my mother. When those days came, I didn't want to make Nikki feel uncomfortable. I would never make her choose between us. I was cordial to my mother, but I didn't stay long at those events. Nikki understood why I couldn't be around my mother's energy. It was a choice, and I chose to be free.

CHAPTER 2- U OF A

My life changed for the better once I started college. I immediately made some wonderful friends who became like a family to me. Allison, who was my roommate, and Shannon, who was my suitemate in my dorm. Along with Heather, Kathy, Ann, and Michael Anne, that are still my friends to this day. I finally felt I that I fit in and was in control of my life. The world was my oyster, and I could do anything!

My first semester started out a bit rough because I didn't know how to study. I had received A's in high school, but I had to do minimal work. I never had to study in order to get good grades. This was not the case for my friends. They had attended private schools or high schools where you could take Advanced Placement (AP) classes. They were accustomed to studying. College classes were not hard for them, but for me it was a challenge.

I finally realized why it was so difficult for me. It turns out I am dyslexic! As a child, I had a hard time with letters, words, and numbers. I just had to take more time or try harder on those things than most kids. However, I now understood the reasons why I had a hard time with testing. I didn't dwell on the difficulty. I knew that I was smart enough to be successful.

But at the end of my first semester, I was placed on academic probation. I never told anyone about it because I was embarrassed. I was also grateful that no one asked me about my grades. I just knew deep down, that I would have better grades the following semester and would get off academic probation. For me, trying harder was a way of life!

The next semester I improved my grades considerably. I had almost a 3.0, which increased my grade point average (GPA). I was now at a passing level of a 2.0 and no longer on academic probation. I was so relieved when I saw my GPA that following semester. I knew that I would not go down that road again. From that point on, my grade continued to improve. I was on the Dean's List almost every semester after that. In order to be on the Dean's list, you had to have over a 3.0 GPA. I was extremely proud of this because I overcame the odds. I pushed myself to learn a different way to study with my dyslexia. Spirit had nudged me again.

I enjoyed college life. Working and hanging out with my friends kept me busy. I didn't think about my past or the traumas I had experience. I was grateful to leave it all behind. Many of my friends didn't know much about my background or my past. The only people that knew were Allison, Shannon, and Ann. Allison was my roommate throughout my years at college and learned more about me and my family. Shannon and I became close. Her family lived in Tucson, and I would always be at her house.

Ann and I became best friends and would take trips to her family's house in Sedona. It took several hours to get there, and we would have deep conversations during those long drives. I became part of her family. I even called her mother "mom." I loved going to Sedona but didn't know why I was so connected there. I realize now that I was very connected to the energy because it is a very spiritual place.

Even though my friends were family, I missed Nikki. We didn't get to see each other very often when I was in college because she had moved to Colorado, but we talked on the phone often. I encouraged her to attend college, which she did several years later at ASU. Nevertheless, I was grateful that I was able to see Steve, Carrie and the boys. They would visit me, or I would have friends drive me to Phoenix to see them. They continued to be a great support system for me. I felt blessed.

After five years, I graduated from the U of A. I had to attend an extra year because I was working 30 hours at The University of Arizona Medical bookstore while going to school. Because I had to work in order to pay for college, I had to take fewer credits each semester. Carrie planned a graduation party for me. She invited my friends, sisters, and my mother. I was surprised that my mother wanted to attend since we had little contact over the years. I later found out from Carrie that Steve made sure that she attended the party. He called her and told her that she needed to be there. My mother gave him many excuses, but he wasn't hearing it. He told her that she would be there, no if's, and's, or but's about it. I never asked him why he did this, but I believe he felt that she needed to honor my achievement.

Even so, I was happy that she was there to show her I was not a failure! I had achieved what she told me that I couldn't do! My mother didn't need to be proud of me because I was proud of myself. The only other person that I wanted to be proud of me was Steve. He had supported me throughout the years, and I didn't want to disappoint him. The highlight of my graduation was when the ceremony ended. Steve was the first one I saw, and he give me a big hug. He told me how proud he was of me and said to look at what I accomplished. I had never heard that before from a parent. It made me cry and happy tears streamed down from my face.

After graduation I had to pack up my belongings because I took a job in California. I also needed to buy a car. I had never owned a car before. I talked to Steve, and he helped me buy a brand-new car. I wasn't interested in a new car, but he insisted. I told him that I didn't have a lot of money, but he told me not to worry about it.

Steve took me to a friend's dealership and told me to pick out a car. I found a small green Dodge Shadow that I loved, and he paid the down-payment for my car. I couldn't believe that he would do this for me.

The following year I paid back the entire amount with interest. I think he was taken back when I gave him the final check. He just looked at me and said, "Thank you." He also told that he was proud of me. I found out later from Carrie that Steve would loan people money and they would never pay him back. He always did it as a gift, but I am sure it was hard.

I should probably mention that Steve never owned a brand-new car. Carrie told me that he wanted to make sure that I would not break down in California. I was taken aback when she told me this. I now understood he why acted the way he did when I repaid him back in full, with interest.

As I reflect on this, I know that this is what a parent would do for a child. I may not have been his child, but I knew that in his heart I truly was his daughter. I was blessed to have Steven as a father figure. I know that Spirit was instrumental in making sure that he was in my life.

Over the next year, I lived in California and Colorado. But my company was sold, and my job was eliminated. This was a blessing in disguise. I was in Arizona for a week getting my wisdom teeth pulled when this happened.

Carrie asked if I wanted to look at the paper for jobs, which I did. I found a perfect job for me, and it was located across the street from U of A. I interviewed with the company in Phoenix and landed the job. I was thrilled to be going back to Tucson because that was where my heart was.

The following week I flew back to Colorado, packed up all my things, and drove to Tucson. I was so excited to start working at Arizona Images. I had been hired on as the manager and buyer of U of A merchandise. I worked with some great people and we all became a family.

As it turned out, a few of my co-workers, Jerry, Julie, and Marikka, believed in the paranormal. We talked about our beliefs and experiences. Jerry believed that he would die young because he had a short lifeline on his palm. He showed me his hand, but I just thought that it was coincidental. Jerry also talked about his dreams being vivid and real. He also saw ghosts, as he was clairvoyant. I told him that I didn't have dreams or saw ghosts any longer. He told me that he knew I had some abilities and they were opening.

At that time, I didn't think anything of it, but I now realize that my abilities were developing. I would hear ringing white noise or high pitch sounds in my ears. This noise would just come and go, and I shrugged it off. I grew up with a constant battle with ear infections, so I thought that these noises were normal. On the contrary, these noises were because of my clairaudience (clear hearing) opening.

I also had the sense of knowing things. This ability is called claircognizance (clear knowing). I would just know when something was going to happen or would feel in my gut that something was off. I always told people, "I listen to my gut." I had a heightened awareness of my clairsentience (clear feeling) too. I could feel people's energy or the energy in a room easily. All of my abilities increased due to the loss of the clairvoyance. Even though I talked about the paranormal, I didn't participate in anything of that nature until a few years later.

When I was 25, I took a trip to New Orleans with Carrie and the boys. I had wanted to visit that city since I was a child. I was excited to finally get to have that experience. When we arrived, we walked the streets to see all the action. I loved the culture, food, and atmosphere. I felt a familiarity with the city, like I had been there before.

We walked to St. Andrews Square, which is the heart of the town. The jazz music playing in the background invites you into the square. The music is infectious and makes you want to dance and sing. While in the square, Carrie told me she wanted to have a tarot card reading. This surprised me because I didn't know that she was interested in spiritual stuff. We never talked about it. As we walked, we came upon the rows of tarot readers. They all had tables and chairs ready to give readings to people. As we passed the rows of tables I paid attention to each reader. I was only drawn to one.

The reader was an older man who wore a turban. He looked to be around the age of 50. I felt a positive energy from him. As we passed his table, I noticed that he wasn't reading for anyone. We walked up and down the rows. When we finished sizing up the readers, Carrie asked me which one I would choose. She said that she wasn't sure which reader to choose and wanted to get my thoughts. I told her the man with the turban was the one that I would choose. So, we walked back by his table and she decided to do a reading with him.

She sat down and paid for her reading. The boys and I stood quietly behind her and listened in. The man shuffled his tarot cards and laid them on the table. He explained what each one meant during the reading. After it was completed the boys asked to have a reading too. Carrie obliged. While the boys were receiving their readings, Carrie asked me if I wanted one too. I kept telling her that it was OK, I didn't want a reading. When the boy's readings were done, they begged me to do a reading with him too. I reluctantly agreed, and Carrie paid for my reading too.

I was not too thrilled about it, but just went along with it. This was my first tarot card reading. I thought, "This should be an interesting experience!" As I sat down, I noticed another tarot deck that was sitting on his table. This tarot deck was old and worn and you could tell that he used it many times. I was curious and asked him about the tarot deck. He was surprised. He picked up the deck and started shuffling. He said that only "old souls" would ask for this tarot deck. He then gave me a look and had a smirk on this face. I wasn't sure what that meant, but I just listened.

While he was laying down the tarot cards, he told me to use my abilities. I didn't comment or gesture I just stared at him and listened. He kept telling me that I knew what he was talking about. Again, I didn't acknowledge him, but I did know what he was talking about. After what I experienced as a child, I told myself that I am not going down that road again! He continued to lay out the cards. The reading was extremely accurate.

He told me about having two different families, and that I would be successful even after a hard childhood. He told me that I would only have three significant romantic relationships, and I knew in my gut that was true. After the reading I thanked him, and he took my hand and looked at me and told me to not forget about my abilities, another nudge from Spirit.

I still have not forgotten his reading or his face. Over the years I have looked for him on several trips back to New Orleans, but with no success. I wanted to thank him for giving me that reading that day. He helped me to open the door up so I could start down the road of my spiritual path.

When I returned home from my trip to New Orleans, I told some of my friends about my reading. They were amazed on how accurate the reading. But they were even more surprised that I was open to having that experience.

My friend Michael Anne was most amazed by the reading. She told me that her mom had a friend in Tucson that was Medium. She claimed that she was "eerily" accurate. Michael Anne said that she had been wanting to get a reading but was scared to go by herself. She asked me to go with her and support her through it. I agreed but wondered what I was getting myself into.

A week later, Michael Anne and I drove to this woman's house. We walked through a patio glass door into a room full of religious statues and pictures. I was overwhelmed by so many religious things in one room. Michael Anne introduced me to this wonderful woman named Lupita. She was in her sixties with big brown eyes and a beautiful smile. Spanish was her native language, and she spoke with an accent.

Lupita escorted Michael Anne into a small room for her reading. I sat on the sofa and waited. I examined this room while I waited. I realized that the energy here was very peaceful. It was light and relaxing, and I felt no fear. After her reading, Michael Anne gave Lupita a hug. Then Lupita looked at me and told me to come back for a reading too. She told me that she knew I was a good person and that she could help me. I knew in my gut that this woman was of the Divine and she was telling me the truth.

As we left Lupita's house, I felt an "urge" to get a reading with her. I went back a week later. Lupita shared very accurate things, and I knew she was telling me the truth. After I left, I knew I would be seeing her again. A nudge from Spirit.

After visiting Lupita, I began researching the spiritual world. I read many books, attended metaphysical events, and started to attract more spiritual friends.

I lived with Kathy, a college friend, during this time. Kathy was always positive and found joy in everything. I loved living with her! Kathy and I shared a three-bedroom duplex. At one point, we needed to find another roommate. Kathy was worried about this, but I told her I would work on finding someone that was "aligned" with us. She knew I was diving into spirituality and that I was going to ask the Universe for help. And that is exactly what I did.

A week later, a woman named Jonel contacted us. Jonel's friend Melissa was moving to Phoenix from New Hampshire and needed a room. Jonel met with us, and we all just clicked. We didn't get to physically meet Melissa, but we felt that Jonel provided a good understanding of who she was. I told Kathy that my gut felt that it would be a good fit. But I also told her to take the night and sleep on it. The following morning Kathy told me that she trusted my judgement. She said that Melissa could be our roommate. I called Jonel and told her that we would rent the room to Melissa. She was happy to hear this news. A nudge from Spirit.

A little over a month later we met Melissa. It was a good fit! It turned out Melissa was very spiritual. She owned a Russian Gypsy Tarot deck and gave us readings. It was easy to use and understand. I was drawn to it. At one point, Melissa told me that she thought I was better at reading her cards than she was! I told her I didn't think so because she had been using them for years, but that comment was the push that I needed. A few weeks later I was in a metaphysical store and saw the same deck. I bought it. Since I knew how the deck worked, I started to give readings to my friends and family. I even persuaded Nikki to buy the same deck when she came to visit me. I enjoyed reading the cards, but it was just for fun. I also continued to see Lupita because her readings were accurate and "authentic." It was the nudge of Spirit.

CHAPTER 3- READINGS FROM LUPITA

Over the years, Lupita told me many accurate things that happened in my life. I received readings from Lupita once or twice a year. I would see her when things in my life were hard, and I couldn't figure out what to do. She always had wise words of wisdom to help me get through the tough times. Each time I saw her, she would lead me into a tiny room. The walls were decorated with many plates. The place came from different countries where her clients were from. This room could barely fit two chairs. There was a desk in there too. I remember seeing Spanish books about "Mediums" on the shelf above the desk, but I had no idea what that meant at the time.

Lupita used Spanish playing cards (cartomancy) to give her readings. She was very superstitious about the cards. She was adamant that I do not cross my arms or legs during the reading. She felt that I would block the energy to receive Spirit's message. I also had to cut the deck in three even amounts. If one pile was off, she would pick up the cards, reshuffle them, and then have me recut them. When I got a reading, I made sure that I would do thing correctly. I didn't want an inaccurate reading! Nonetheless, there was an instance that I felt I might have done one of these things to make the reading inaccurate.

In December 2000, Lupita told me about a new job that I was going to receive. It would pay more money and provide me security. She also told me that I was going to move to Phoenix, and I would be happy living there. I didn't understand this. I loved my current job. I had left Arizona Images the year before to work at the University of Arizona bookstore. I was excited because I could work on my master's degree while I worked there. I bought merchandise and managed the store at McKale Center. I had wonderful friends that worked with me. Jody, Erica, Stacey and Marisol were like family to me. I wasn't looking for a new job! I thought to myself she must be mistaken!

Lupita then talked about my family. She told me that there were hard times ahead. She said that a male family member was going to pass away. I first thought of my grandfather because he had been ill. Then she told me that my mom was not "thinking right." I thought to myself, my mother has always been this way, but who knows, I haven't talked to her in many years! Lastly, she told me I would meet a man that was into politics, and I would have a romantic relationship with him.

When I left the reading, I was perplexed. I was confused about the entire reading, and I kept wondering if I had crossed my legs! Turns out I didn't cross my legs during the reading because everything she told me all came to fruition.

In January 2001, I drove to California with Steve, Carrie, and the boys to see a U of A game. While I was there, I saw Nikki too. We met up for lunch, and she had a surprise for me. She brought my Uncle Nick to meet us too. They were living together. I hadn't seen him in years.

His appearance surprised me because he looked older than my grandfather, his dad. We caught up on our lives and laughed a lot. I didn't know it at that time, but that was the last time I would see Uncle Nick. Less than two months later, he unexpectedly passed away of a stroke at the age of 48.

I realized that the male family member Lupita said would pass away was my Uncle Nick, not my grandfather. After I returned home from California, I planned to visit my grandfather in Greece. I had not seen him in years, and I was happy to spend time with him.

My grandfather was sad that gout prevented him from attending my Uncle Nick's funeral. I was happy that I had been at the funeral. This made him feel better too. My visit also helped to keep his mind off the funeral. During my visit, I asked my grandfather to tell me stories of his life. He was a good storyteller because he could remember great details. He even drove me to the place where he was born, and I saw where he lived. The visit with him was amazing. I cherished every moment.

After my visit with my grandfather, I was happy to start the fall semester of school. This meant that football season would start the following month. As usual, I saw Steve and Carrie for the first football game. During that visit I found out that Carrie was not doing well. Steve told me that she was not thinking clearly, and I wouldn't be seeing them very often. I told him that I understood and that I would step back from the family until she was better.

Once he left, I thought back to Lupita's reading. I realized that Carrie was the "mom" that she was talking about! Lupita's prediction about Carrie was accurate. I was stunned. A few weeks later Carrie's "thoughts" unfortunately worsened. At one point she met up with me and told me to stay away from her family. I was shocked. I didn't know what she was talking about! I hadn't seen or talked to anyone in the family. I didn't know what to do.

The next day I called Steve. I told him what had transpired the night before because I was extremely worried about Carrie. He listened and told me that she wasn't getting better. I promised him that I would continue to step back and not contact anyone in the family. I just wanted her to get better! After I got off the phone it felt like I was losing my family again.

The girls at McKale were a blessing! They cheered me up and helped me to realize that situation had nothing to do with me. As time passed, I focused my energy on my work and classes. I was sad that they were not in my life, but I knew in my gut that there was a reason for this. I wasn't sure why, but I knew the nudge from Spirit was all I needed to help me get through this pain.

My job was the only thing that made me happy. When I was working, the McKale girls kept me busy and made me laugh. They were amazing, and it helped me tremendously. But Spirit had another plan in mind, and change was on the horizon.

It was late October 2001, and I was getting ready for basketball season to start. My boss, Debby, called and told me that a man named Matt would be stopping by. He was a buyer for the Team Shop, a company under the umbrella of the Phoenix Suns and the Arizona Diamondbacks. I had heard of Matt's name before from the vendors that we both worked with. I also knew that he had gone to school at the U of A.

Matt was in Tucson because the Suns were playing an exhibition game at McKale. Matt came down from Phoenix to see how the Suns merchandise was selling that night. We talked about buying merchandise, vendors, and life. We got to know each other and had a good time. Before he left, he handed me his business card and told me to contact him if I ever needed anything. I thought that this was very nice, but I didn't intend on contacting him as he was a busy man. But Spirit had something different in mind!

The following month I ended up sending Matt an email. I wanted to purchase a cap that he sold because the Diamondbacks had won the World Series. He responded and told me where to get the cap and hoped things were well. I was happy that I heard from him. I ordered the cap, and I didn't expect to hear from him again.

Then February 2002 rolls in, and I received another email from Matt. I was surprised because he had already responded to my original email about the cap. I didn't understand why he was writing to me again. Again, he told me where to get the cap. Then I read the last line of the email and almost fell off my chair! He wanted to know if I would be interested in a buying job! I quickly thought back to Lupita's reading about receiving a new job, and it took my breath away. However, what I found out later from Matt was how Spirit made it happen.

Matt was working with a buyer named Kim. Kim was pregnant and had to quit to go on complete bedrest. He needed to hire someone right away because the season was going to start in few weeks. Plus, it had become so busy because of World Series win that he really needed two buyers!

Matt said he was really stressed out because he wanted to find the right person. He was a spiritual man and knew that he needed to work with the Universe to manifest the right buyer. Matt asked the Universe to bring the right person to work under him. He said that asked daily.

While Matt was asking for help, my work computer started to act a bit strange. This was not normal, so I contacted our tech person. He investigated it and said there was a slight glitch, but it should be running fine. After that night my computer ran fine with no other issues. However, when it was experiencing the glitch, my computer resent my original email to Matt! Somehow, the email had been saved in my drafts folder, which I had never used before. This was the only email that was resent due to the glitch. This small event ended up turning my life upside down. A nudge from Spirit.

I read and reread Matt's email and knew I had to respond that I was interested. I replied, and we planned to meet in Phoenix on a Sunday later that month. It was my only day off that month because so many sports seasons were overlapping. I met up with Matt and his boss Bob for lunch. I immediately had a connection with both men. I felt like I just fit in. I knew in my gut that I would be hired.

A month later I received a call from Val, the hiring manager for the Suns and Diamondbacks. She was trying to reach my boss, Debby, for reference, but accidently called me instead. We talked a bit, and I found out that she went to U of A too. We just felt like we knew each other. It was another nudge from Spirit.

The following day Bob called me, and he offered me the job. I accepted. I would be moving to Phoenix in less than a month. Before I left Tucson, I saw Lupita to tell her the good news. She was thrilled and told me to come see her whenever I was in Tucson. I told her that I would make sure to come and see her. As promised, I continued to see Lupita for readings once a year. She was always happy to see me and would tell me to visit her more often. Lupita's goodbyes always entailed the saying, "Have peace in your heart."

As I reflect on Lupita today, I now understand why I was led to see her for over 20 years. She was a very religious person, and Spirit wanted to show me that I could use my abilities for "the good." Lupita worked with God, her guides, and Angels, or "white light" as I like to call it. Intrinsically, I knew that if Lupita, who was a devoted Catholic, was giving readings, then this could not be evil. Spirit had found a way to help me think differently about the paranormal. Even though I experienced the dark side of things as a child, I could choose to work in the "white light" and help others.

Seeing Lupita was a huge breakthrough for me. Her readings and guidance helped me to realize that I could be a Medium. I knew that I could be like her and just work in the "white light." She encouraged me to talk with God, the Angels, and Archangels on any matter. She told me to trust my gut in any situation because it told the truth. Lupita also told me that I was wise beyond my years and would help others in this world. I always felt at peace when I left her house. Her words, wisdom, encouragement, and essence were the things that I needed to help pave my way down this spiritual road.

CHAPTER 4- THE BALLPARK & JERRY
2002

After I accepted the job at the Team Shop, I had to tell the McKale girls the news. They were sad that I was leaving, but happy that I had this opportunity. I went home and started to pack because I was leaving in less than a month. I talked to Nikki later that night, and she was excited for me. However, I was sad that I couldn't tell Steve and Carrie the good news too. My relationship with them was, unfortunately, non-existent.

The following weekend I drove up to Phoenix and met up with Julie. We had worked together at Arizona Images, and she had been living in Phoenix for a few years now. We went apartment hunting, and I found a perfect place that was just 10 minutes from the ballpark. I was thrilled. Julie and I ate a late lunch and made plans to meet up when I moved to Phoenix.

As I was driving back to Tucson, I received some good news. Erica told me that she and her parents, Hope and Cisco, wanted to help me move to Phoenix. I felt so blessed because I was close to her and her parents. Three weeks later, they helped me move. Cisco drove the U-Haul, and Hope, Erica and I followed in our separate cars. We arrived at my apartment a few hours later and unloaded everything. Then I took them to have dinner at the ballpark. The restaurant overlooked the field. They were all huge baseball fans and loved it. While I ate dinner, I looked at the field and couldn't believe that I would be working there in just two days! After we said our goodbyes, I knew the next chapter of my life was about to start and it was going to be an interesting one. Julie came over the next day to help me unpack and to catch up. She was so excited that I was finally in Phoenix too.

I started my new job on April 16. I enjoyed my job tremendously. There were so many people that I loved working with, including Matt, Bob, Nancy, and Val. Thanks to this job, I was fortunate to travel all over the country. I met buyers from other teams, and several of us became so close that we were like a family. When I was not working, I saw Julie and Jerry. We attended baseball games together and had a lot of fun.

I still used my gypsy cards, and I bought a tarot deck too. I also drove to Tucson to get a reading from Lupita to make sure that things were on track. During this reading, she told me that I would soon meet a man with dark hair who worked in politics. Lupita told me that I had to be open to having a relationship with him. I thanked her and was excited about this new opportunity awaiting.

October came, and the baseball season had ended. I met a dark-haired man named Daniel who lived next door to me. I started to hang out with him and a few other friends who lived in our apartment complex. We would go to the movies, have dinner, and hang out at each other's apartments. Soon, Daniel and I began hanging out exclusively because we got along great. I found out that he worked in politics, loved the Phoenix Suns, and was younger than me. I wasn't interested in Daniel romantically because I felt that he was too young for me. That changed a month later when I started to date him. Lupita's prediction was correct.

Prior to dating Daniel, I had only had one other significant relationship, with Michael. Daniel was different than Michael, and he turned out to be the second significant romantic relationship in my life. Daniel may have been younger than me, but he was very intelligent and a gentle soul. I introduced him to Julie and her husband, Eric, one night at dinner. We had a great meal and enjoyed each other's company. Julie and Eric told me that they were happy that I was finally dating someone. I told them I was happy too, and we made plans to get together soon. My life was very happy and fulfilled, but things changed the following month.

A few days before Christmas, I received some sad news. I had been sleeping, but something made me wake up to check my phone. It was almost midnight when I woke up. I had a voicemail from Nikki. I listened to the voicemail and couldn't believe what she said. Aunt Penny (AP), our favorite aunt, had unexpectedly passed away from a heart attack at the age of 61. I was in shock because I just talked to AP a few weeks prior. I didn't want to call back Nikki because it was late, so I went back to bed with tears rolling down my eyes.

I started to talk out loud to AP. I told her that she was in a better place now and that I loved her. Immediately after I said these words the blinds in my room started to move! It was like a gust of wind had come in, but the windows were closed. Somehow, I knew in my gut that this was her. It was a nudge from Spirit.

The next morning, I called Nikki to tell her what happened with my blinds. She felt that this was AP too telling us that she was okay. This made us happy. Even so, because it was the holidays it was a tough week due to her passing. I kept my mind busy with Daniel, work, and travel for the next month.

2003

February arrived, and things seemed to become brighter. My sister Michelle called me and invited me to Nikki's surprise birthday party in Las Vegas. She and her friends were throwing the party and wanted me to attend. I told her I wasn't sure if I could make it since Daniel's birthday was the day after Nikki's. I told her I would find out what he wanted to do for his birthday and that I would get back to her.

I talked to Daniel, and he thought it would be a great idea to drive to Las Vegas and surprise Nikki for her birthday. Then we could celebrate his birthday on our way back home by skiing in Flagstaff, Arizona. I loved this idea and I called Michelle to let her know we were coming.

A week later, Daniel and I drove to Las Vegas on Valentine' Day to arrive that night. Nikki was completely surprised that we came for her birthday. She had heard about Daniel, but this was her first time meeting him. After meeting him, Nikki thought that he was a good match for me. Daniel and I enjoyed the weekend with her and then drove to Flagstaff to ski.

This was my first-time skiing and Daniel was very patient with me. He showed me how to ski, and I picked it up quickly. We had a wonderful time skiing and we enjoyed the time we spent with each other too.

In April, Daniel and I decided to move in together. A week after we moved in together, we went on a cruise with his family. We all had a great time. I loved being around his family. Daniel and I bonded more, and we loved being around each other. I felt grateful that I went out on a limb and took the chance to date him. My life seemed to be coming together bit by bit, but the one thing that I missed was Steve, Carrie, and the boys.

This became evident one day during work. Nancy and I started to discuss our families. I teared up and told her that I missed my family more since being around Daniel's family. She encouraged me to write an email to Steve, telling him how I felt. I took her advice and wrote that email.

I told Steve that I missed the family and gave him an update on my life, including my job and dating Daniel. I told him I was sad because Daniel and I were talking about marriage and I wanted him to walk me down the aisle. I told him that I hoped everyone was well. I felt happy after I sent the email. The next day Steve replied and said he wanted to meet up for dinner. I was so excited about this news and shared it with Nancy, Daniel, and Julie. They were all happy for me.

A few days later I met Steve at the same fish restaurant where we ate at before I went to college. We were both happy to see each other and to catch up on each other's lives. He said that the boys were at college. He also that Carrie was traveling and would be home next week. I asked how everyone was. He said that the boys were good. He had let the family know that he was having dinner with me, and that they said to tell me "hi."

Then I asked if Carrie was getting better. Steve told me that she was working with a therapist and was getting better one step at a time. I told him I was happy to hear this news, and I left it at that. We talked about my life in Phoenix, and Steve was happy about me dating Daniel. He knew his name from being in the political scene. After dinner, Steve told me that he would have lunch with me soon since his office was close to the ballpark. He also told me that he would give the boys my number so they could catch up with me too. I was so happy to hear this news. It was a blessing from the Spirit.

In May, Julie and I went to Jerry's wedding. Jerry had been dating Kelly on and off for several years. We both felt that she was not the girl for him, but they had a son together. Jerry knew our thoughts, but he also knew we would support him regardless.

The wedding was not your typical wedding to say the least. Their families did not seem to like each other and didn't talk to one another. They were split her side versus his side. During the wedding ceremony when the pastor asked if anyone objected to the wedding, a loud noise erupted. This noise came out of the blue, and everyone was looking around to see where it came from. It was a cacophony of birds chirping. Julie and I just looked at each other. We knew that this was a sign from Spirit!

Nevertheless, Jerry and Kelly were married. We hoped for the best for Jerry's sake.

Daniel and I began having some trouble with our relationship a month later. He was having a hard time finding a political job in Arizona. He started to look for jobs outside of Arizona, which caused stress on both of us. I told him that I wanted him to be happy, and he needed to do what was best for him. That night I read my gypsy cards and saw a breakup in a relationship. I thought I read them wrong and went to bed. A nudge from Spirit.

Daniel started to apply for political jobs around the country a week later. This was hard because we both knew that I wouldn't leave my dream job. I had always wanted to work in baseball, and I finally achieved my dream. We just had to wait and see what was in store for us.

While all of this was happening, I saw one of the boys for lunch. Steven was happy to see me, and we caught up on our lives. We had a great time and I told him I would see him in Boston next year when I was there for work. I was happy about reconnecting, and I felt that I had a piece of my family back.

The happiness was short lived because my relationship with Daniel abruptly ended. Daniel was offered a job in Indiana and would be moving there soon. This was one of the toughest and saddest times for me. I moved from our apartment to another one in the apartment complex. I felt like I was getting a divorce from Daniel, and it was very depressing. Not to mention I was in complete shock that this was happening. I wasn't listening to the nudge from Spirit!

The following weekend the McKale girls came and stayed with me to try and cheer me up. Then Julie, Val, and Nancy had dinner with me different nights. Melissa stayed with me right after that. Everyone helped me to laugh and remember who I was. I was so blessed to have my friends around me during these tough couple of weeks.

At the beginning of September my sister Michelle came to visit me to cheer me up. We had made plans to hang out and drive to Tucson to have readings from Lupita. When I arrived at the airport, she had a surprise for me. Nikki came with her. I was overjoyed! I should have suspected something because Michelle had called me a week before asking me to add another person to the reading with Lupita. She told me that her friend from Phoenix really needed a reading too and wanted to come with us. I thought that this was a bit odd, but I didn't question it. I called Lupita and added another reading to her list.

Nikki was very fond of Lupita and loved to get readings from her too. Michelle had only heard of Lupita and was excited to finally receive a reading from her. The next day we drove to Tucson to see Lupita. She was happy to see all of us and gave us readings. She told me that my relationship with Daniel was complete and to let it go. She said that I would see the blessings later. I didn't understand what she meant at that time, but I do now. My relationship with Daniel would not have lasted because of our different paths. Since he was in politics his career would have suffered because of my career of being a Medium. It was hard to hear, but I trusted Lupita and her advice. I knew I had to let it go. After my sisters left, I tried to keep myself busy with work. My job was a blessing because I enjoyed it and it gave me focus.

While all of this was happening, Jerry called me and that was a great distraction. He told me that his marriage was not working. He gave me some of the brief details and wanted to meet me to get my thoughts. I told him that I would call Julie too and schedule a dinner. Then we could all discuss our thoughts. He agreed.

He asked how I was doing, and I told him about my breakup with Daniel. He felt bad that he was telling me his drama when I was having a hard time myself. I told him not to worry about it because it gave me something else to focus on. A week later we all met up. Jerry told us what was happening in his marriage. After listening, Julie and I told him that the best thing to do was to separate. He appreciated our thoughts and we left the restaurant that night. After that night, I left him a few messages, but I didn't hear back from him. I thought to myself he needs a bit of time and would hear from him soon, I left it at that.

It was now October, and I met Steve for lunch. I gave him the update on my relationship with Daniel. He was sad to hear this news and encouraged me to date other people. I asked about Carrie, and he told me that she was fine. He added nothing more. We talked the usual topics: the boys, sports, and fishing. We made plans to have lunch soon and left.

I called Julie right after the lunch, and she told me that she had something to show me. I told her to come the following day as I was excited to see what the surprise was. Julie came over and brought a small white teacup poodle that fit in her hand. She had named her "Faith." The tiny dog was running around all over my apartment and balcony. Julie told me that she wanted to bring Faith over to cheer me up because I was depressed about Daniel. We also talked about Jerry. Neither one of us had heard from him. We tried to call him, but there with no answer. We left him a message to call us back. Then we continued to play with Faith and enjoyed the day.

A few weeks later, I finally heard back from Jerry. He told me that he was separating from Kelly and moving into an apartment. He said that he needed time to really think about his decision and hadn't talked to anyone. I told him that I understood, and I thought that this was the best decision. He asked me to relay the news to Julie too. We made plans to meet up after the holidays. After I hung up, I immediately called Julie to give her the update on Jerry. She wasn't surprised. I told her that we would all meet up after the holidays and she agreed.

2004

The holidays came and went, and it was now the middle of January. I met up with Jerry and Julie for dinner. Jerry told us about his new apartment and that he was doing well at work. His life was better since separating from Kelly. He said that he felt like he made the right choice. We were both happy for him.

Then the conversation switched to me. They wanted to know how things had been going. I was happy to share that I was better, and I was starting to do more things. I told them that I was traveling to New Orleans in a few weeks with my sister Michelle. We both wanted to experience Mardi Gras. They were happy that I was starting to live life again. After dinner we planned to meet up for a baseball game in April.

Michelle and I met in New Orleans for Mardi Gras a month later. Neither of us had been there during this festive time, so we were excited to experience it. We immersed ourselves into the festivities right away. We stayed in the Garden District and saw how the community embraced this holiday. It was family oriented, with children collecting beads, stuffed animals, coconuts etc. The children had homemade ladders with a box at the top to sit in as they collected these trinkets. The floats were incredible, as were the bands and the jazz music. The atmosphere was loving and happy. It was infectious.

At one point, we decided to get our tarot cards read in St. Andrews Square. We read with a woman who gave us accurate messages. She told me that my heart was broken and that I had to heal from that relationship. She also told me there was going to be a change with my job. After we left, I thought it was a bit odd regarding a change with my job, but I let it go. It was a nudge from Spirit.

Mardi Gras was the next day. Michelle and I rented a spot-on top of a balcony which was located on Bourbon Street. I was grateful that we did this because Bourbon Street was overwhelming. It was packed from every corner of the street with people. I was grateful that I was not in the thick of the crowd and could see everything from above. As the night went on, we thoroughly enjoyed the festivities and left the next morning.

April was upon us and baseball season was in full swing. I met up with Julie and Jerry for a baseball game. We all caught up on our lives. They wanted to know how Mardi Gras was and if I would go back for it. I told them I would go back to experience it again without a doubt. We continued to chat and enjoyed the night. It was a great night for baseball.

Later that month I saw Steve for lunch, and we caught up on our lives. He told me that Carrie was the same and there was nothing new to share. Steve gave me an update on the boys. He said Larry would be in Phoenix next month and to give him call to meet up for lunch. So, a month a later I had lunch with Larry. We caught up on each other's lives, which made me happy.

Several months went by and life was good. I was supposed to meet up with Jerry at the end of July, but I had to cancel because my water heater broke. He called me the following month and said that he needed to talk. His life was not working out for the best, and he was thinking of getting a divorce.

He told me that he had lost his wedding ring. Jerry was very spiritual and felt that this was a sign from God. I told him not to overthink it and that I would plan another dinner for us. I called Julie and let her know the news. We planned the dinner.

A week later we met up, and Jerry told us that he knew that he had to get a divorce. He said he had been asking God to give him a sign about his marriage and then 2 weeks later he lost his wedding ring. He said that it was time, and he was going to move forward with this decision. He also told us that he was going to move the following month. He wanted to be closer to his work. We supported his decision and told him that we would be there if he needed us.

September arrived, and I had planned a surgery to finally fix my nose. I was having a very hard time breathing out of it. Not to mention that shards of bone were starting to protrude out of it. Daniel had recently moved back to Phoenix to work on a political campaign, and I asked him to help take care of me after surgery. We had remained friends after our relationship had ended. Daniel took me to surgery, and I had the procedure done.

After the surgery I found out that my nose was completely shattered. All the doctor could do was shave down the protruding parts and fix the deviated septum. He said that my nose was not stable because of how it grew back, thus he couldn't do anything else for it. Nevertheless, whatever he did to fix my nose helped me to finally breathe out of it. The procedure was life changing. Deciding to fix that old would become the best decision that I made.

A few months went by and November rolled in. Jerry called me to tell me that he was finally settling into his new apartment and things were getting better. I told him I was planning an after Christmas party with all the Arizona Images people. He said that he would come, but I would have to remind him. I agreed. I also let him know that I was here if he needed to talk. After hanging up with Jerry, I called Julie to give her the update on him. I also told her that he was coming to the party. She was happy about. We wished each other a Happy Thanksgiving and said we would catch up at the party the following month.

December was in our midst, and I was getting ready for the party. I called Jerry on the 22^{nd,} to remind him of the party that was taking place on the 27th. He said that he was going to be there. Jerry told me that he was going to see his family for Christmas with his son but would be back.

His family lived a few hours away. He promised me that he would be on time for the party and wouldn't forget. Then he wished me a Merry Christmas. Who knew that would be the last time I would speak with him!

When the night of the party arrived, I tried calling him several times and left voicemails. I didn't hear back from him. I thought this was strange because he promised me that he would be there. I then thought about everything that was happening in his life. Jerry must have changed his mind and is still with his family. I left it at that. After the holidays I tried calling Jerry on his cell several times, but it always went straight to voicemail. Again, I felt this was odd, but I knew Jerry would get back to me. As the weeks went on, I still had not heard from him. I became a bit concerned, but I knew Jerry. I knew he would contact me when he was ready to talk.

2005

It was now the second week of February, and it was going to be Jerry's birthday. I was frustrated because I hadn't heard from him. I decided to call him at work. I located his work number and left him a message. I told him I was very worried and that he had better give me a call. As I hung up, I remember saying to myself, "Where are you Jerry?"

Two days later I received a call at work. It was one of Jerry's co-workers. She knew who I was because he would talk about going to watch baseball games with me. She knew that I worked at the ballpark and called the main line to get ahold of me. She preceded to tell me that he passed away on Christmas Eve night in a tragic accident. She felt awful that I didn't know and gave me her condolences. I was completely stunned and in shock because he was only 28.

Jerry had been like a brother to me, and it hit me to the core of my being. I immediately started to call our friends from Arizona Images to let them know this awful news. I was so shaken up that I had to leave work early. I was in complete shock.

I left my apartment a few days later, and I saw a sparrow in my hallway. I thought this was strange because I never had seen one there before. The bird kept looking at me and chirping. It was not scared of me at all. I looked to see if the bird might be injured, but it wasn't. It kept chirping and staring at me. I eventually had to leave. When I returned later that evening, I saw the little bird again. It saw me and came up to me and started to chirp again. I went inside to get bread for the bird, but when I came back out it was gone. I never saw that bird again. Somehow, I knew in my gut that this was a sign from Jerry. Spirit was giving me a nudge.

I remained shocked of Jerry's passing over the next several months. At one point I drove to Tucson to get some clarity. I saw Lupita to get a reading about Jerry. She told me that Jerry didn't suffer and that he was on the Other Side. She told me that he would be with me. She also confirmed that the bird was a sign from him. I was grateful to know this, and she made me feel at peace. It was a blessing.

When I got home, I sent a letter to Jerry's mom to give her my condolences. I told her how much Jerry meant to me and that he would be missed. She sent me back a letter thanking me. She also told me that Jerry thought highly of Julie and me. I was happy to hear these words as I felt it was a piece of Jerry speaking to me.

I still thought of Jerry, and it was bittersweet. When I saw Julie, we would reminisce about Jerry and how he would make us laugh. When I was watching a baseball game at the ballpark, I always thought of him and missed him. He never seemed too far from my thoughts. As the weeks turned into months, things began to brighten up. I started to get out more and live life. That changed a short time later.

I heard some disturbing news at work. My five-year anniversary with Team Shop was coming up when I found out that our division was sold. The prediction from the woman in New Orleans was accurate! Matt decided to leave and start his own company, so the head buying position was open. Nonetheless the new company XP Apparel which was based in Denver did not hire me for the buyer position. They had their own buyers and didn't feel they needed me. When I heard this news, I was devastated. I couldn't believe that this was happening. I wasn't sure what to do, but I knew Lupita could offer wise words of wisdom.

The following day I called Lupita to set up an appointment. I drove to Tucson a few days later. Lupita gave me a reading and told me not to worry. Lupita felt that I would have a job soon, I just had to be patient. She told me that I would be happy with this new job. This made me feel relief.

I left her house with peace in my heart. I knew something was on the horizon.

As I was leaving Tucson, I called Nikki to give her the update on my job and the reading. Nikki was so supportive and drove down to see me the following week. I was grateful to see her because she was a good distraction while I was job hunting. She cheered me up and told me to not worry about the job. Nikki reminded me of Lupita's reading which helped me to be more positive about this job situation.

After Nikki left, I couldn't find anything in the buying field. I took a part time job helping Daniel on his political campaign. He knew what had happened with my job and wanted to help. Working for him this allowed me to have a bit of income while I still looked for a full-time job. I did my best to stay positive and told Spirit that I wanted my old buying job back. I felt that I had more work that needed to be done with that job. It was my claircognizance kicking in and I trusted it. A nudge from Spirit.

A month later I received a call from a man named Aaron. He was one of the men that bought the division of Team Shop. Aaron wanted to meet me because he realized that he needed to hire a buyer in Arizona. I agreed to meet him for dinner. After the call I told Daniel the news and he was thrilled for me. He gave me advice on how to negotiate, for which I was grateful.

I met Aaron later that evening, and I asked him why he didn't hire me in the beginning. He told me that since they were buyers themselves, they felt they could handle it. But they realized that had made a huge error in thinking. None of the buyers knew the computer system or the Phoenix business market. He desperately needed me. We talked some more, and he wanted to hire me on the spot. I told him to please send me an email with all the details on the job offer. He agreed and we left.

The following day I received and email with the job offer. I had Daniel read it. He was good with negotiations and with fine print. When Daniel read it, he saw a small detail in the contract that would not give me as much money as I expected. So, I sent Aaron an email about it. I know that Aaron was surprised when I called out this detail because he asked me if I was working with an attorney! Nevertheless, he fixed the wording. I ended up making more money than before I was laid off. I was so grateful that

Daniel was there to help me with reading the contract. Not to mention giving me a temp job during my job hunt. A week later I returned to my old job as the head buyer. Spirit had heard my plea and blessed me!

CHAPTER 5- THE FAN
2006

My new job with XP Apparel came with a new office location. It was now on ground level of the ballpark, right outside of the opposing team's bullpen. When I walked in each day, I passed the field. I always smiled when I walked by. And I loved working with Patsy, the new director. She and I felt a kinship from the beginning and became fast friends. I learned that Patsy was spiritual. She was clairvoyant and clairsentient too. We loved to talk about ghosts, paranormal, mediums, etc. We always seemed to be on the same page. We worked hard together but had many laughs in between. I finally felt at peace, and things started to come together. But this only lasted for a few weeks. I received another nudge from Spirit.

In February, after working at the ballpark for two months, I moved into a new condo. I was excited about my new place. It felt serene. I just loved coming home, sitting on my couch and looking around. I couldn't believe that I owned this condo! It was such a blessing, but a few weeks later something changed. Fear started to set in.

One night, I woke up and noticed that the light in the guest room was turned on. I lived alone; no one could have turned the light on. The light was part of a fan that I rarely used. I got up and turned it off. I didn't think much of it. I was tired and went back to bed. A few nights later, it happened again! This time, the light and fan were both on! This continued to happen every few nights.

I tried to use logic to figure it out. My condo was brand new, so the electrical part of things should've been fine. But maybe there might be a loose wire which was triggering this? I wasn't sure, so I called Nikki to get her thoughts. She advised me to contact an electrician, you know, just to be safe. So, I arranged for someone to come out and check. The electrician couldn't find anything wrong with it!

At this point, I figured it had to be paranormal related. Fear grew as I thought back to my childhood home and the lights that flickered on and off. I felt so uneasy and starting to ask God to help. I didn't want to relive my childhood nightmares again. I asked that only things of the "white light," be allowed in my house. I hoped that this would take care of it, but that was wishful thinking on my part. I had no idea it was a nudge from Spirit!

The fan and light continued to turn on. Since I had asked, I knew that whatever was turning on the light and fan had to be of the "white light." If you ask for good you get good. It's the Law of Attraction. So, my mind started to wander. I started to think, maybe this could be Jerry? Maybe he was letting me know that he was doing alright. I wasn't sure, but I knew I needed to find out.

My schedule prevented me from driving down to Tucson to see Lupita. So, after a few weeks of research, I found a local Medium and made an appointment. I asked her about the fan and light. She said that she felt it was a family member who passed was turning on the fan. This person wanted me to know everyone is doing well on the Other Side and to now let it go.

She then told tell me that I had abilities, just like the reader in New Orleans! She also said that I needed to start to work with them. She suggested that I start to work with my Spirit Guide, Theodore. A guide is a spiritual being that works with you and guides you on Earth. Your guide is with you your entire life. When she finished the reading, I thanked her and left. I was relived she told me that a family member was turning my fan on!

I took the Medium's advice and let the fan issues go. I knew in my gut that Jerry was doing okay too. I also started to talk with my guide who I nicknamed "Teddy." I can say it was a bit strange at first, but I trusted the process and asked him to help me. I'm sure after all these years he was jumping for joy that I finally started to work with him! Once I started, neither the fan nor the light came on. What a relief! Several months passed and life was back to normal. But Spirit had other plans in store for me.

One evening, as Nikki and I were catching up during a phone call, we were reminiscing about AP. AP was spiritual and had had a gentle soul. She had been like a mom to us, and we both missed her terribly. AP loved to visit Nikki in California and go to the beach. And even though she lived in another state, we both talked to her regularly.

Nikki and I believed that she had died of a broken heart. We both felt that she was in a better place and wasn't suffering anymore. We chatted a bit more, but it was late, so I told Nikki I was heading to bed. As I passed my guest room, I saw that the fan was on! I couldn't believe it. I ran and called Nikki. She was in disbelief too. We concurred that it was AP who was turning the fan on. She wanted us to know that she heard our conversation regarding her. I walked back to the guest room and began speaking to AP. I let her know that it was okay to turn my light and fan on. Then I turned off the fan and left the room.

I talked to Nikki for another 10 minutes. She told me to check the fan one more time before we hung up. I walked by the room again, and the fan was on! AP had been turning the light and fan on! I was relieved and thankful that it was her. I told her that I wasn't scared and that she was welcome to visit anytime. But I told her that she could only visit the guest room, because otherwise I would be scared! She must have heard me because it was a few months before she turned the light or fan on again.

Once the fan dilemma had been figured out, life was easy and peaceful for a few years. However, I started getting nudges or inklings that I needed to take classes to hone my abilities. This was my claircognizance kicking in. I ignored these thoughts and let them pass. I was busy with my job, and I didn't have any extra time. My life was all about work. I enjoyed my job, but I didn't have a personal life. Spirit provided a wakeup call to remind me!

2009

It was December, and I received a call from my uncle Nicko in Greece. He said that my grandfather was on his deathbed. I just couldn't take another person passing, so I asked Spirit to keep him alive so I could see him one last time. I did this for several days. Spirit heard me because my grandfather miraculously recovered. I spoke to my grandfather a week later. I promised him that I would see him in a few months, so he needed to get stronger. My Uncle Nicko told me that my grandfather willed himself to become stronger because he knew I was coming.

2010

I went to visit my grandfather in May. As soon as I saw him, I knew he was not well. His health was worsening by the minute. I was grateful that I made this visit because I knew this was the last time, I would see him. During my visit, my grandfather had his good and bad days. On the good days he was alert and himself. I asked him to retell the stories of his life, which I loved. On the bad days, he would just stare at me.

But there were moments during his bad days when he became alert and told me that AP and Uncle Nick were standing right beside me. When he said this, I knew that his time on Earth was almost complete.

I also helped my Uncle Nicko during this visit. I went through all my grandfather's papers, including his will and financial papers. My grandfather lived in America most of his life, so the paperwork was in English. Uncle Nicko knew some English, but the language in the paperwork was too advanced for him to understand properly. I worked on many things to get everything in order for my uncle.

Despite the sadness of this trip, I enjoyed my time with my uncle. We talked about spirituality, and I told him about AP and the fan. Uncle Nicko believes in the paranormal and is clairvoyant too. So, he wasn't surprised when I told him about the dream that I had the night before.

I dreamt of Nikki. She had a ring and told me that she was getting married. As he listened, his eyes grew in amazement. He told me that Nikki had left a message last night! We immediately called her. She told us that she was engaged! I was shocked because this came out of the blue. I told her about my dream, and she couldn't believe it. It was a nudge from Spirit.

The days passed quickly, and I knew my time with my grandfather was coming to an end. I cherished the good days I spent with him. I also knew this would be the last time I saw him. On my final day in Greece, I had to tell my grandfather a "final goodbye." It was hard, but I was glad it was a "bad" day for him. He was out of it and not himself. The previous day had been a "good" day, and for that I will always be grateful. I will keep the memories of that trip forever. I cannot thank Spirit enough for giving me the opportunity to visit him one last time.

I returned home and went back to working a lot of hours. This kept my mind busy and prevented me from thinking too much about my grandfather. I did, however, consider the nudges that I received from Spirit. I thought about the dream I had in Greece, as well as AP and Uncle Nick's visits with my grandfather. I knew that I needed to pay more attention to these nudges. I wasn't quite sure why, but I felt that something shifted in me that gave me clarity or awareness. It was a nudge from Spirit.

In July, I saw a flyer about an automatic writing class. I knew nothing about automatic writing, but I felt a needed to attend. I listened to the nudge from Spirit and signed up. I sent an email to Joan, the instructor, to find out more about the class. She was thrilled to hear that I was interested in the class. Joan told me that the class was designed to allow inspired thoughts, pictures, words, etc. to come through from pencil to paper. These thoughts would come from the Divine, and the person was just a vessel putting them on paper. The person doesn't physically move the pencil, it moves on its own. This sounded interesting, but I wasn't sure why I felt that I needed to take this class. I just trusted this nudge and waited for the first class.

Ten people attended the class. Joan introduced herself and provided us with information. She then took us through a meditation. After the meditation, it was time to start. Joan instructed us to put the tip of our pencil to the paper and just let things flow. Immediately I heard scribbling on papers, but nothing was happening to my paper! I thought to myself, "Why did I come to this class? It's a waste of my time!" After 10 minutes, everyone described what they drew on their papers. I was the only one that didn't have anything on their paper! Joan came by my table and told me not to worry. She said that we would do another round and I could try again. I just nodded at her. I thought, "Nothing will happen to my paper."

We started the next round a few minutes later. I put my pencil to paper and just waited for something to happen. To my amazement, the pencil moved in my hand! The pencil made the letter "M" followed by a long line and then the letter "Y". At this point I was shocked that this was happening. I looked again, and my pencil was still moving. I don't know why, but in my gut, I knew that it was Mother Mary. I was shocked and didn't say anything.

Joan walked by my table and looked at my paper. She saw the M and the Y and said that she felt that "Mother Mary" might be coming through to me. After she said this, the woman on the other side of my table said, "YES, I see her standing right behind her." I was shocked! I hadn't told them what I thought. I couldn't believe that they felt it was her too! When I left the class that night, I didn't know what to think.

I tried to figure out why Mother Mary was coming to me. I wasn't religious, and I never prayed to her, so why me? I was a bit stumped, but I let it go and went to sleep that night. The next day I tried working with my automatic writing skills again. My pencil immediately started to write. The name "Mary" appeared on my paper. I asked if this was Mother Mary, and my pencil wrote YES! This freaked me out a little to say the least!

I asked her why she was coming to me. The pencil moved, and she said that she was one of my guides. It was hard to believe, but somehow, I knew it was true. I continued to write with Mother Mary for weeks. I never told anyone that I was connecting in with her. I just received information from her and kept it a secret.

September arrived, and I prepared to go fishing with Nikki in San Diego. I knew that I needed to tell her about my experience and connection with Mother Mary. I had not shared this news with her yet because I felt she needed to hear it "in person." So, I decided that I would share this news with her the first night. I was nervous about sharing this, and I kept thinking, "If it is hard for me to believe that this is happening, how is Nikki going to feel?" I just had to trust that she would believe me.

Nikki picked me up from the airport in the middle of the afternoon. We checked into our hotel and went to get something to eat. After dinner, we decided to go back to the hotel room and rest because we had to be up early the next morning to go fishing. It took me awhile, but I finally got the courage up to start the conversation.

I told Nikki to sit down because I needed to tell her something. I prefaced it with that she needed "to hear me out" before she said anything. I began to tell her about the automatic writing class that I took. I explained that the person that came through to me on paper was Mother Mary. As I told her this, I noticed the look on her face. She looked at me like I was crazy! I explained to her that I didn't know how it worked but that it just did. Then I demonstrated how automatic writing works. As I connected to my pencil, it started to move. Words started to appear on the paper. "This is Mother Mary, and I am going to answer your sister's question. Nikki wants to know, why are we here on Earth?" Then she gave her explanation.

As I wrote, Nikki watched the words appear on the paper. She gasped and almost fell off her chair. I didn't know what to think. Nikki told me that, while she drove to San Diego, she asked God, "Why are we here on Earth?" She was shocked that I was able to answer her question. Nikki believed this was real because there was no way I could know about her conversation with God. She said, "I really thought that I might need to take you to the mental hospital, but I know you are telling me the truth, and I believe you!" I was so happy to hear this because she knew it was real. I finally could talk to someone about this!

We discussed it some more but decided to go to bed because it was getting late. When we woke up, Nikki told me she had a restless night. She was still shocked from Mother Mary's message. I told her I could relate, but I had had a few weeks to absorb the shock. Then I told her, "let it go" that way we concentrate on having fun fishing. And that's exactly what we did. We caught several fish that day.

The next day, Nikki dropped me off at the airport and told me to continue to use automatic writing with Mother Mary. I agreed and told her I would let her know if Mother Mary had anything else to tell her. We said our goodbyes, and I flew home. After the San Diego trip, I continued to work with Mother Mary through automatic writing. I was quietly enjoying life, but then I received another nudge from Spirit.

After working for XP Apparel for several years, I started to notice that I would develop laryngitis every few weeks. At first, it would last for only a day or two. But it started to take longer and longer for my voice to fully come back. Sometimes it would last for up to two weeks. It was so noticeable that my coworkers and vendors commented on it. It got to the point that I had to see a doctor to get a prescription or shot of steroids. I didn't know it at that time, but Spirit was trying to give me a nudge.

When I was having voice issues, I was very stressed from work. It became apparent that my company was having money issues. The vendors I bought from started to hold the merchandise that I had purchased. They told me that they were not getting paid, so they could not ship my order. I decided I had to have a conversation with my bosses, Aaron and James. It was hard for me to bring up, but I made them aware of what the vendors told me. They listened and said that there were some cash flow issues. They told me not to worry because it was starting to clear up, but I knew in my gut that something was off. And I was right. A few months later, the company filed for bankruptcy.

Another company, Gameday Merchandising, bought the company. I thought the situation would improve and my voice would get better, but it became worse. Gameday Merchandising kept all the employees, and we continued work as normal. I worked hard to get the merchandise that had not shipped before. It was a stressful process, and I continued to lose my voice. Spirit kept nudging as a warning, but I wasn't listening.

I received a big wake-up call a few months later. Aaron called me to tell me some bad news. He said that the new owner was going to lay me off because I lived in Phoenix. He wanted all the buyers to work together in Denver. Aaron had told the owner that I didn't want to move to Denver. He had known this from the first day he hired me several years prior. Aaron said his hands were tied and the only thing I could do was to contact the new owner to discuss it.

That is exactly what I did. I hung up the phone with Aaron and dialed the owner's number. He was surprised I called but allowed me to share my thoughts about the layoff. Somehow, I managed to talk the owner into keeping me as a buyer in Phoenix. The tradeoff was that I would make a lot less money and have a change in job duties. He told me that he was going to split half of my job duties between two other buyers in Denver. I was not thrilled with the situation, but I was happy because I was able to keep my job and could stay in Phoenix.

The transition was a struggle to say the least. I was miserable because the other buyers had never bought for a professional sports team before. I was an experienced sports team buyer. I had purchased for the Phoenix teams for almost 10 years and knew what was needed. Unfortunately, my advice or insight was ignored. The new buyers didn't understand what merchandise to buy for the teams and that affected my job. This went on for several months. I was unhappy and became extremely negative. The stress affected me so severely that I developed serious health issues.

2011

    In February, I was diagnosed with bronchitis and extreme laryngitis. The doctor put me on bed rest for a week. He also told me that I could not return to my office because the dirt from the field was severely affecting my lungs. I had to work from home until the new grass for the season was laid down. It was two weeks before my voice returned. I continued to work from home for another month and a half. Physically, I was blessed because I was in a healthy environment. Mentally, I continued to be irritated and felt negatively about my job. Three days after I finally returned to my office, I received another wakeup call came from Spirit.

    It was April 7, the day before opening day at the ballpark. Unbeknownst to me, the owner sent a man named Tim, whom I had never met, to Phoenix. He met with me and told me that I was being laid off. I was stunned. I tried negotiating with him, but this time I couldn't talk my way back into staying. I was crushed. I couldn't understand why this was happening to me again! I thought, "How many times can a person be laid off at a job?" I didn't realize that my negative thinking had created the job layoff. But I knew what to do, I called Lupita for an appointment. I drove to Tucson the next day for a reading with Lupita. She told me another job was around the corner. That put me at ease.

    When I returned to Phoenix, I had to get my bags packed because I was leaving for Las Vegas to attend Nikki's wedding. I tried to be excited for Nikki, but I was stressed out about the job situation. However, I put my game face on and made sure that I did what Nikki needed me to do. The wedding was amazing, and Nikki looked beautiful. I was so happy because she deserved this.

    After the wedding I stayed with Nikki for a few weeks to get my mind clear about the job. I felt blessed that she gave me this opportunity. When I returned home a few weeks later, Lupita's prediction came to pass. I was hired on to be a buyer for a department store. This was something I never thought I would be doing, but it was a buying job and it was in Phoenix. When I took the job, I thought that it would be temporary. I fully expected Gameday Merchandising to call me again. Boy was I wrong! I had no idea what was in store for me. But Spirit did, and I was in for a big surprise!

CHAPTER 6- SPIRITUAL AWAKENING
2011

I started my new job at the department store in mid-May. From the very first day I felt like I wanted to quit. But I knew I had to give it a chance. I couldn't believe how old their computers and computer systems were! And the people and the environment were toxic! Everyone working there was miserable, including me.

I started as an assistant buyer for the shoe department. After three months, I was promoted to be a buyer in the Juniors department. I thought that it would be a good move, but it was a complete disaster. I had to learn a different computer system, and the girl training me gave me only one day of training. There were piles beyond piles of papers too. I had to work from scratch to clean it up. I also ended up working for a terrible boss named Kim. She did not like me because I had a background in buying, and she wasn't used to that. To say this was a nightmare was an understatement. I couldn't believe that this job was ten times worse than my job at Gameday Merchandising.

On a positive note, I shared an assistant name Marie with the two other buyers. She was my saving grace. Marie was the only friend at that job. She taught me how to use the computer systems, Juniors buying, and the backend of this company. She had worked there for over 10 years and knew the inside scoop. She gave me insight and taught me how to work around things. She saw that I was being treated unfairly compared to the other buyers. Marie couldn't understand why Kim didn't like me, especially since I did my work and my sales were up.

As our friendship grew, I found out that Marie was very spiritual. We talked about spirituality and the paranormal. She told me that I needed to talk to her friend Suzie who worked in the dress department. Our different schedules made it almost impossible to connect with her. But Spirit made sure that we connected a month later.

As the holiday season rolled in, my schedule changed a bit. I was in my cubicle when Suzie walked in. She introduced herself and said that she knew that I was into spirituality. We started talking and clicked right away.

Suzie told me about a spiritual group that she attended once a month. The group would talk about spiritual topics and meditate. She invited me to attend the following month. Suzie wanted me to meet her friend Joy who hosted the group. I agreed but was a bit nervous because I wasn't sure what to expect. However, I was excited to be around more spiritual people.

Next month, I met up with Suzie and followed her to Joy's house. Suzie introduced us, and I immediately felt a kinship with Joy. I knew that I was supposed to be in this group. I also met Roseanne, Suzie's best friend, and I felt a kindship with her too! I called this group, the "YAYA" group because it reminded me of the movie the *Sisterhood of the Traveling Pants*.

The women in the group were a sisterhood. Everyone wanted to expand, grow, and learn about spirituality. Joy was very enlightened and had been working with spirituality for over 30 years. She was a Medium, reiki master, energy healer, astrologist, and shaman. Spirit had our paths cross because I could learn from her. After that night, I regularly met with the group each month for several years. Not only did I learn several things from Joy, but we had a bond. She was able to give me guidance on many things as I grew spiritually.

2012

When January arrived, I received a call at work from my Uncle Nicko. My grandfather had passed peacefully in the night. The call shocked me because my grandfather's health had been stable for the last year. I was so grateful that I was able to see him before he passed. I was unable to attend his funeral, but I was there in spirit! I received a sign about him. A few days after hearing the news. AP turned the light and the fan on for several days in a row. I was happy because I knew that my grandfather had made it to the Other Side. I thanked her for giving me the signs and told her to take care of him. I smiled and sent them my love.

In February, I asked Kim if I could use the vacation time I had accrued. I had received the time during the company's blackout days and couldn't take any vacation before this. Blackout days were a period when employees were not allowed to take time off. The days included November through most of January.

When I asked Kim about using my days, I couldn't believe what she told me. She refused and would not honor any of my accrued time. Kim said that I needed to take the time prior to the beginning of February. I found out that I was going to lose a week of vacation. It was a shock. I told her that the blackout days prevented me from taking time off before February. She just said those were the rules and that was that. I tried to contact people at the corporate office, but they didn't have an HR department. This was very typical of this company. I was extremely upset to lose my vacation time as I worked hard for it. I became even more miserable at my job, and my negative thinking increased. However, Spirit helped me to receive some time, at the end of the year.

It was April, and the light in my guest room turned on again. I was glad that AP was connecting with me because I hadn't heard from her in a while. When I went to turn the light off, it burnt out. I thought this was strange. I had changed the bulb because I noticed that it was dim the last time, she turned it on. I went to the store and bought a new one to replace it. I told AP that I had a new bulb, and she could start to use it again. The next day the light came back on, but it immediately blew out. This was not a coincidence. I knew that there had to be a reason for it.

After I pondered it for a bit, I realized that AP was trying to train my grandfather on how to turn the light on. My grandfather had been an electrician, so turning the light on would be right up his alley! I went back to the store and bought another bulb to replace it again. I told AP that the light bulb was fixed, and she could use it again. I should have been more specific about what I told her!

Guess what happened again the following day? The same thing! I was completely frustrated by this. I told AP that grandpa was not allowed to turn the light on because he burns them out. I then explained to my grandfather that I was sorry, but he was not allowed to touch any of the electrical things in my house. I also told him that he should be the best trained at this because you are the electrician! Then I just laughed. How ironic is it that an electrician was burning out the light bulbs? After my conversation with them that night, my light bulb didn't burn out for several years!

As many months passed, I struggled at my dead-end job. Each day seemed to be harder than the day before. I hated to go to work. I constantly searched for other jobs, but nothing was available in Phoenix. I was in tears most of the time because I felt stuck and helpless. I could not see light at the end of the tunnel, only darkness looked back at me. Attending the YAYA group was the only thing that made me happy. I felt that I was a part of a group and that these women cared about me.

In October, Val wanted to go to the Arizona State Fair. It was a yearly tradition for us. Plus, Val wanted to catch up with me regarding the job search. We didn't feel like riding that many rides, so we looked at the exhibits instead. We had never done this before, so it was a new experience.

There were so many things to see. We walked around and came upon a booth which had two women giving psychic readings. Val asked me to go with her to get a reading, which surprised me. Val knew I saw Lupita for readings, but she never felt the need to get one. When she suggested it, I thought that it was odd, but told her that I would go with her. So, we waited in line. It turns out that she was in the line for the mother while I was in line for the daughter. While I waited, a family sitting next to me started up a conversation. They told me that they saw the daughter a year ago and that she had been very accurate. They shared a few more details about her and told me that her name was Buffy.

After about 15 minutes, it was my turn. I walked into a small makeshift booth with a curtain. Buffy was sitting down with some tarot cards on a table. She told me that she was a "gypsy" and that she has read tarot cards for many years. Buffy asked me my question and then shuffled my cards. As she shuffled, she told me about my aura (energy around the body). Buffy told me that my aura was red and gray, but she saw gold at the top. I had no idea what this meant, so I asked her. She said that a person normally has many more colors, but that my aura was very muddy and murky. She said that I need to get an "energy cleaning." I asked her what this meant, and she said it cleans out stuck energy in your body. Buffy gave me her business card and told me to call her if I wanted to do this. Buffy preceded to give me a reading that was accurate. After the session, I was taken back and told Val what Buffy had said. I wasn't sure why, but I knew

I had to get this energy cleaning. Val told me to think it over and go with my gut. That is exactly what I did.

I pondered it for a few days. While I pondered, I researched auras. I discovered that red was associated with anger, gray was associated with sadness or depression, and gold was associated with the Spirit. I realized that the colors of my aura correlated with situations in my life. I went back and forth in my mind, considering whether or not to do the energy cleaning. I replayed Val's words, "Go with your gut." I contacted Buffy and made an appointment to have her conduct the energy cleaning on me.

I met up with Buffy a few days later. She said that she would work with my energy and clean up each layer of my chakras (energy points in the body). This would include cleaning, restoring, and praying for each chakra. She said that when she would be working on me tonight that I might feel sensations in my body. Buffy also gave me a tall round chakra candle to burn during this cleaning. This candle was made up of 7 different colors. Each color represented one of the chakras. When I got home, I would have to burn the chakra candle continuously. This would also help to clear the old stuck energy that I had in my body. I took the candle thanked her and left.

When I got home, I burned the candle as instructed. I wasn't sure what to expect, but I trusted the process. I started to feel a strange sensation in my body and knew that she had started to work on me. I became tired and went to bed. When I woke up the next morning, I felt a bit better. I checked on the candle and it was still burning. There wasn't a dent in it! I asked myself how long would it take for the candle to burn? Well, it took over a week of continuously burning.

What transpired during the candle burning was unreal! As it burned, the candle split in half, like it had been cut down the middle! I had never seen any candle burn like this before. The best way to describe is to say it was like a Phoenix rising out of the ashes. I was stunned by how it burnt, but I knew it was working. Each day, I felt better, both physically and emotionally. After many sessions and money, I felt back to my old self. AP kept turning the light or fan on. I knew that she was happy that I received the clearing. I felt very connected to her, and my house was very peaceful. I knew that something inside me shifted, and it was a good thing.

I know now that Spirit led me to Buffy to get my mind and body clear. The energy clearing helped me to recognize how strong my abilities really were. I didn't realize this before. Spirit also taught me another lesson, which was to always trust your gut! Even though Buffy had ultimately helped me, I felt that something was off. My claircognizance was giving me the sign. Buffy charged me an extreme amount of money for the energy clearing. At that time, I had no idea of what it would cost but I do now! It was a great lesson because I can now be sympathetic and understanding to clients who come to see me after they have experienced a similar situation. I am grateful that I met her because it was a pivotal turning point for me. I shed the old for the authentic me to come through.

At the beginning of November, my job required the buyers to work in the department stores for the holiday season. I was not looking forward to this, but thoughts about seeing Nikki for Christmas kept me going. That was the only thing that made me happy because this job was beyond toxic.

I lost my voice two days before Thanksgiving Day. Losing my voice was a pattern for me, but I wasn't paying attention. Even though I didn't have a voice, Kim still made me work in the stores. Calling out sick was not an option unless I had a doctor's note. It was the day before Thanksgiving Day, and I couldn't get in to see the doctor or get a doctor's note. That meant I had to work Black Friday and the entire weekend with no voice! I still couldn't believe that she would make me work the busiest weekend without a voice. I knew she didn't have my best interest at heart, but I made the most out of it and tried my best to help people. After that weekend, I was severely sick. I was out of the office for several days.

I came back with a doctor's note, which had restrictions on what I could and couldn't do. Kim gave me a nasty look when she read the note. She was upset that I couldn't be around the public, which meant I couldn't work in the stores. Nonetheless, she still had me come into the office on the weekends to work. I knew that she was being spiteful, but I was grateful I wasn't working in the stores. After another week of working constantly, I got sicker. I ended up having bronchitis. I was put on bed rest by the doctor until after New Year's Day. This was the blessing Spirit provided to me. I received over two weeks off on paid medical leave, and it felt like a vacation from work!

While I was on bed rest, Marie helped me with my job. She kept me in the loop on what was going on at the office. She told me that Kim was upset I was off during the busiest season, but she could not do anything about it because I was on medical leave. I was blessed that Marie kept me in the loop. She had my back. She was my true friend.

While I recovered from my bronchitis, I received a text from Michael Anne. She told me that Lupita was very ill and had stage four cancer. Michael Anne said that she had just a few weeks to live. When I heard this news, I was devastated. I wished that I was well enough to go see her, but my bronchitis prevented me from being around anyone, especially someone with cancer. I asked God to give her healing from any pain and help her through this transition. A few days before Christmas, Lupita peacefully passed away at her home at the age of 89. I was sad to hear this news, but I was happy that she was no longer suffering from the effects of cancer.

I thought about all the wonderful memories that I had of her. I remember her beautiful soul, words of wisdom, and the readings that she gave me over the years. I thanked her for always helping me as the tears rolled down my face. I knew I was blessed to have met such a beautiful soul in this lifetime. I told God to take care of her and wished her well on the Other Side. After the holidays were over, I returned to work. Kim didn't say too much to me when she saw me. I worked hard and did my job as usual, but I knew in my gut that something was brewing. Another nudge from Spirit.

2013

In February, I noticed that Kim was behaving even worse toward me than she had before. Soon, I was told by a new boss, Jody, that they were transferring me to her department in a few days. I was in tears. Not only had they took my vacation days away, now they were going to send me to clean up another department's mess! I would also be leaving my friend Marie who always had my back. The only blessing that came out of it was that I didn't have to work for Kim any longer. I moved to the Plus Size department, and I never talked to Kim again. Spirit gave me the biggest blessing in disguise!

There was a tremendous amount of work to be cleaned up in the Plus Size department, and I was exhausted. I jumped into that department with no training from anyone. Nonetheless, I figured it out and cleaned up the mess within a few weeks. Even though I didn't have to work under Kim, I still hated going to work each day. I would come home in tears every day. The environment was so extremely toxic that I felt I was sucked dry of any positivity left in me.

I knew I had to make a change but didn't know how to do it. I continually asked Spirit to give me the opportunity to go back to work at Gameday Merchandising, but it never happened. As the weeks went by, I became more and more depressed. I tried to look for other buying jobs, but there was nothing in Phoenix. I reached out to several of my old friends in baseball, but the jobs available were in other states. I considered one in California, but it would not be available until fall. At this point, I just resigned myself to the fact that at least I had a job to pay my bills and I didn't have to work under Kim. I gave Spirit gratitude for this job and started to see things as being more positive. Once I changed my thoughts about my job, something shifted. I didn't know it at that time, but Spirit was opening a door for me.

At the end of February, I received a call from a friend named Bobbi. I knew her from Team Shop, and we would often walk at a park on Friday nights. Bobbi was very supportive and wanted to help. She called to tell me that she would share something with me on the next walk. Bobbi loved to talk about spirituality, and I assumed it had something to do with that. We planned our usual Friday night walk and met up.

Bobbi told me about a workshop that she attended. The workshop was about manifestation and how to bring what you want into your life. She told me about the Law of Attraction and how our thoughts become things. I knew a bit about this because my old boss, Matt, had told me about the book, *The Secret* a few years prior. This book talked about manifesting and how to get what you want out of life. I had never read it, but I was hearing about it again! After walking with Bobbi, I knew that Spirit wanted me to hear this message. Ironically, it had been made into a movie that had just been released on video. I rented the video and watched it. The message was simple: "What you think is what you get." It works like a magnet. The

Universe brings to you what you think, no matter if it is a good or bad thought. The choice is yours.

After watching the video, I understood why I had been laid off from my job! Duh, it was me and my negative thinking! I had told Spirit that I was unhappy with my sports job. So, the layoffs happened because of my negative thoughts. I realized at that moment that the Voice from Spirit was telling me, "Change Your Thoughts!" I finally received the message loud and clear, but for some reason I still didn't start working on changing them yet. Spirit found another way to make me hear that message again!

One morning in March, I bumped into my friend Trina at work. She worked in a different department, so I didn't see her very often. Trina talked about a book that she just read called *The Game of Life and How you Play It*. She said that the book was amazing, and I had to read it. I ordered the book off the internet and waited for it to arrive. The book arrived a week later, on the same day that Nikki was in town to see me. Nikki had some work to do for her business, so I told her I would just read this book until she was finished.

Once I started to read it, I couldn't put the book down. I read the whole thing in an hour. I knew at that moment I had to change my ways. The Voice of Spirit was again telling me to think differently! The book impressed me so much, that I made Nikki take it to read on the plane. From that day on, I started to change the way I thought. I would give daily gratitude's to Spirit for what I had, which included my job. When I chose to be happy and be positive, a door opened right before my eyes.

At the end of March, I received some free World Baseball Classic tickets from a friend. The game was held at Chase Field, the Diamondbacks' ballpark and my old stomping ground. I invited Bobbi to go with me to thank her for being supportive. I also wanted to share my new thinking and attitude with her. Bobbi and I met at the ballpark and were excited to see each other. We sat down, talked, and watched the game. At one-point Bobbi wanted to get some food. She asked me if I wanted to go with her and see the Team Store. That was the biggest store that I bought merchandise for. I don't know why, but I told her I would go with her. We walked around, Bobbi ate her food, and then we walked to the Team Store.

When I walked in, I literally ran into my old boss, James. He lived in Canada, and it was very unusual that he was working that day. We started to talk, and I asked him if he needed another buyer. He told me that the buying was still in Denver and knew that I didn't want to move there. James said he would think about having a buyer in Phoenix again. He said that he would get back to me in a few days about his decision. I thanked him, and Bobbi and I walked back to our seats. Bobbi told me that whatever happened, at least you will know what direction that you must go in. Either the direction would be going back to work at Gameday Merchandising or regrouping and letting go of the idea of returning to this job. I agreed with her and left it up to Spirit.

A few days went by and James sent an email saying that he didn't have a buying job in Phoenix but wished me well. I was disappointed after reading the email, but I told Spirit that I am finally letting go of that job. I knew in my gut that something better was on the horizon. I continued to give gratitude daily and worked on manifesting a new job. I remained positive and continued to search for jobs. I knew that something would come up, but that I just needed to be patient. I trusted Spirit and couldn't wait to see what was going to be coming to me. Boy, did I get a surprise!

One night in May, I checked my email. James had sent a message asking me if I still wanted a buying job. He discussed how some things had changed since he last saw me in March. James let me know that his current buyer in Denver was leaving and moving to Florida. He was currently looking for another buyer to replace him. James asked me to let him know if I still was interested in working for him. I immediately responded back to him. I told him I would only be interested if the job was in Phoenix. I immediately received a reply from James. He told me "YES" that I could live in Phoenix and the buying job would be for two Major League baseball teams. I was thrilled to hear this news. Tears ran down my face, and I thanked Spirit for the opportunity.

James called me the following day to work out the details. I was hired on to start in June. I had manifested my old buying job back! This job was better because I didn't have to work with other buyers, and it came with more money! I finally realized that I had to let go of wanting my old job back to receive an updated version of it! The nudges from Spirit helped me to receive this new job!

After I accepted the job, I had to tell Jody that I was leaving. We were in New York for a week of buying when it happened. I called her on her cell and told her I had to talk to her. Normally, I would have waited to tell her the news, but I had to be in Washington, D.C., for a buying meeting two weeks later. I didn't have a day to spare!

Jody met me during a break with my vendor. I told her then and there that I was quitting. She looked completely stunned and asked me if I was unhappy with her. I told her that it had nothing to do with her. I explained that I had the opportunity to go back to my old company and buy sports merchandise again, which was my passion. I felt bad because Jody was a good person and treated me fairly. I didn't want her to think that I was leaving because of her. I also told her why I had to give my notice now. She understood and wished me well.

Later that evening, I was on cloud nine walking through the streets of New York! I bought myself an ice cream and could not stop smiling. As I walked, I continued to thank Spirit for my new job. I remember I walked for miles sharing the fantastic news with Nikki, Julie, Marie, and Bobbi. I finally arrived back at my hotel a few hours later. When I went to bed, I had a hard time sleeping because I was so excited to go back and work in sports again! Thank You Spirit!

The last two weeks at the department went by fast, and I was thrilled. I trained a new buyer, and I made sure that she had everything that she needed so it would be an easy transition. On the last day, I bought some donuts to share with some of the staff. I bought Marie her favorite bear claw donut and thanked her for always being there for me. I knew that we would always be friends and told her I would see her soon. I saw Suzie and gave her a donut and she just laughed. Since we saw each other monthly at the YAYA group, she told me that she would see me next month.

The last person I gave a donut too was Trina. I told her that her book recommendation put me on this new path. I thanked her and told her that we would keep in touch. The day flew by, and I was ecstatic. I was grateful because I never saw Kim again, which was fine with me. Once I walked out of those doors, I never looked back, and that chapter was finally closed for good!

The next day I returned to Gameday Merchandising. I immediately felt back at home in my old office on the ground floor of the ballpark. And it was great seeing my old coworkers. I received my laptop, phone, and badge, then I got everything in order because I had to go to Washington, D.C., the next morning. When I arrived in D.C., I met up with my bosses, James and Aaron. They introduced me to Mary and Jeff, who were my liaisons for the Washington Nationals. We all clicked, and I felt that I knew them before. They showed me several buying lines. I gave my recommendations, and they loved what I choose. I was back in my groove, and it was like I had never left. We worked the entire day plus two more after that. I flew home and had a lot of work to do, but I didn't mind because I loved my job!

Over the next few months, I worked hard, and the sales increased. My bosses and teams were happy with the results. I was happy too because I was finally back in the environment that I loved. It is amazing that when you love what you do everything just seems to be more positive too!

In October, the baseball season ended. The job was going well, and I continued to give gratitude to Spirit. I was happy and life was grand, but then something odd started to occur. I constantly saw the same numbers all day long. I would see either 11:11, 1:11, or 1234. If that didn't happen, then I would wake up around 3 am. It was very odd. I knew that I wasn't looking for these numbers, they just appeared. This continued for a few weeks, and I thought that it was coincidental. Who knew that it was not!

I know now that my Angels were showing me these numbers. They were trying to get my attention and to spiritually wake me up. The Angels will show you a sequence of numbers which have a meaning. If you go to the internet and look up Angel Numbers, you will be given a meaning for each number or sequence of numbers. Also, the hour between 3 am and 4 am this is called the witching hour. This is when the veil between Earth and the Other Side is thin, and it is easier for our Loved Ones to connect in with us.

After I started to see the number sequences, I brushed it off that it was just in my head. Well, that was a mistake. When Spirit wants you to know something, they will get your attention. And that is exactly what I experienced. One night I awoke around 3 and saw a man's floating head staring at me! I lived alone and this terrified me! I screamed, jumped up, and turned the light on. I looked back, and it was gone. Since I have rarely dreamt since I was a child, I knew that I wasn't dreaming. I also knew logically that I saw it with my own eyes! I didn't know what to think, but I talked myself into thinking it was a dream so I could go back to bed.

A week later, the same things happened at 3 am! I saw the same head staring at me just a few inches from my face. Again, I screamed, turned the light on, and saw nothing there. I shook my head. I couldn't believe that this was happening again! I didn't know what to do. I was so petrified that I couldn't move. I eventually climbed back into my bed with my covers over my head. This time, though, I left the light on! I thought to myself that this floating head was NOT going to scare me again! I tried to drift off to sleep, but I couldn't stop thinking about it!

The next morning, I called Nikki and told her about these episodes. We tried to figure out who this floating head belonged too. Eventually we concluded that it was my Uncle Nick because he was the jokester. Once I hung up the phone with Nikki I immediately went to my bedroom. In a stern voice, I told Uncle Nick that you are NOT to come in my room at night! I let him know that if he wanted to visit, he had to go to the guest bedroom! I was not only exhausted from a sleepless night, but I didn't want to be a part of his shenanigans either.

In November, I flew to Orlando for a weeklong baseball conference. I arrived a few days early to see Julie who now lived there. While we were at baggage claim, Julie asked me how things have been going. I shared that I had been seeing "floating heads" at night and if I were to wake up screaming, now you know what it is about! Using her fantastic sarcastic humor, she said, "Well, I'll let Eric know too so he won't get his gun out!!" Eric, her husband, is a retired police officer and is all about safety. We both started to laugh! It was so good to see her again!

When I returned to Phoenix, the floating heads disappeared, but the numbers kept popping up! I saw them day and night for several weeks.

Seeing them caused me to become annoyed and frustrated. One night something woke me up. I looked at the clock and saw it was 1:11am! I wanted to scream. I was so frustrated by this. I got out of bed, and I went straight to my computer. I wanted to find out why I was seeing these numbers. I typed in "seeing numbers 1111" and wouldn't you know it there were several articles, written about these numbers! "Wow" is all I could say. I thought to myself "I am not crazy after all!"

I read the articles for several hours. What I found fascinated me. I realized that I was experiencing a "spiritual awakening." My angels were waking me up to give me messages. They wanted me to understand why we are here on Earth. Once I read this, I searched the internet for spiritual and psychic classes. I decided that I wanted to understand my abilities. I also wanted to find a Mediumship teacher. And Spirit led me right to a website with all this information!

I discovered that Harmony was offering these types of classes in January. I would have to send an email to find out if there were any available seats. I bookmarked the webpage and went back to bed for a bit. I was exhausted and overwhelmed by what I discovered. When I woke, I contemplated sending that email, but only for a short time. Teddy, my guide, told me that I needed to contact them! Then, he revealed that he was the floating head!

I was shocked. I asked Teddy why he would scare me like that. He told me that I was ignoring all the signs, and I needed a big wakeup call! Well I couldn't argue with him as it DID get my attention! Once I found this out, I felt bad that I blamed my Uncle Nick and apologized to him. Then, I sent an email to Harmony. I secretly hoped that the class was full. However, I wasn't going to tell Teddy that! A day later I received a response. There was an open seat! Teddy told me I needed to sign up for that seat, which I ultimately did. I wasn't sure what was in store, but I wasn't going to worry about it. The class didn't start until the end of January and I had several weeks before I had to think about it. It was a nudge from Spirit.

PART II

CHAPTER 1- CLASSES, FRIENDS, & CHICKS WITH SPIRITUAL GIFTS

2014

January arrived, and it was time to finally start the Beginning Mediumship class. The day the class was to start, I thought about it constantly. But when I went home that night, I decided that I was not going to go. I kept thinking, "I really don't want to open the door to bad things!" With that in my mind, I sat on the couch and turned on the television.

In a stern voice, I heard Teddy say, "YOU ARE GOING!" I was in shock because Teddy never spoke to me this way. I told him that I didn't want to go and that it would be a waste of my time. He kept saying "YOU ARE GOING!" I finally gave in and said "FINE." I proceeded to tell him that if I didn't like this class, I would not go back the following week! He agreed and I reluctantly left the house.

I drove to this small red brick building and parked in the back. The class was held at a place called Harmony, a Spiritualist church. I had never been to a spiritualist church before, so I didn't know what to expect. I entered the building and sat down on a green fabric chair that was one of many in a circle. A woman named Sheila was the class instructor. I introduced myself to her. She seemed very nice which made me feel at ease.

I looked around the circle and noted there was 13 of us. Everyone "looked" normal. I guess I wasn't sure what to expect but I was grateful that I wasn't surrounded by weirdos! I noted that the energy of these people felt very peaceful. Sheila introduced herself to the group and told us that she trained at the Arthur Finley College (AFC) in the United Kingdom. I had never heard of the school but learned that it is a prestigious place to study your abilities.

After her introduction we all went around the circle and introduced ourselves. I was sitting next to Kim, a clairvoyant and a healer. During the class we learned about the different "clairs" or abilities that we have. This was the first time I had heard about these abilities. I realized that I had experienced clairvoyance as a child. I also discovered that I had the ability of clairaudience, clairsentient, and claircognizance too. I learned that everyone has abilities, but that there are different levels of ability. I loved learning this fascinating new material.

Once the class was over, I realized that Teddy was right! He was probably chuckling to himself because he knew that I would attend the class every week. I didn't know it that night, but the class ended up changing my life.

After a few classes, I started to immerse myself more into the spiritual world. I wanted to understand my abilities and learn how to use them. I went on Amazon and ordered spiritual books. I was ready to purchase an order when I noticed a recommended book called *Intuitive Studies* by Gordon Smith." I figured it couldn't hurt to order it, so I added it to my cart too. A few days later, 10 books that I ordered arrived. I read them veraciously because there was so much to learn. I wasn't only reading books; I was researching spirituality online too. I was inundated with spiritual information!

While I sifted through all this information, I realized that I was more spiritual than religious. I started to revisit the religious beliefs that I grew up with. As a child, I questioned why we had to go to church to talk to God. I knew that He was all around us, so we should be able talk to God anytime. I also considered what I thought about the church as an adult. I never felt the urge to go to church, but I did feel the urge to talk to God. I realized that God was not a "Him" or person in the sky. God was an "energy" or "Spirit."

My thoughts turned to the Bible. I felt that the Bible was man made, and I questioned why there were so many variations of the same book. I wondered why stories were presented differently in different Bibles. I asked myself, "Shouldn't their stories all be same?"

I also pondered how people treated each other. I wanted to know why people couldn't see each other as the same. I felt that we were all "One" and came from the same place. My mind began to reel. I tried to figure how why some people would hurt others or animals? I questioned why God would punish us and send us to a place called Hell? The more I thought, the more questions arose!

As I researched, I was able to let go of these questions because I found the answers. I realized that religion was man made whereas spirituality is within you. I like to say that you are a piece of the God, Higher Power, Universe, or Spirit. This is what made sense to me, and I finally felt at peace. It was the breakthrough that I needed. I had always been working with Spirit, but now I knew what label to use!

I called Nikki to tell her about my abilities and my enlightenment of spirituality. She was very supportive and told me to keep learning more. A few days later she called me and told me that she talked to our mom about my abilities. She said that our great grandmother was spiritual and had abilities too. I was surprised by this because my mother never talked about her. The only thing I knew of her was that I had a teacup saucer that belonged to her. I am not sure why I ended up with it, but I always cherished it. I realized it was a nudge from Spirit.

My deep dive into understanding spirituality propelled me further into learning. I received this gut feeling (claircognizance) to work and practice my abilities outside of class. So, one night in the beginning of March, I started to research spiritual mentors online. I found a mentor named Jeanne. Jeanne lived in Minnesota, but she agreed to take me on as a student and help me develop my abilities. We would Skype each week, and my abilities developed quickly. She told me that she had never mentored someone with my level of abilities.

Jeanne also told me that I was an "old soul" and had been Medium in many lifetimes. My soul was tapping into these lifetimes and my abilities were expanding quickly because of this. I was reluctant to believe this when she told me. I thought, "Really? Me?" I didn't think my abilities were that heightened; I just knew I had to keep practicing.

Jeannie continued to push me to work deeper with my abilities. After less than a month of working together, she assigned me homework. She wanted me to start reading for other people. Hearing this petrified me. I told her that I didn't know who to read for. I explained to her that the only my sister and the people in Sheila's class knew I was studying this. Jeanne didn't want to hear it. She just shook her head. She told me to read for the people in my class or to find an online chat room and read people there. I told her that I would figure something out and would complete the homework before our call the following week.

When the call ended, I had a sick feeling in my stomach. I didn't want to do this, but I knew I had to. I decided my safest bet was to read for the people in Sheila's class. So, I decided at the next class I would go out on a limb and ask.

I didn't have to wait for the next class to start my homework. During a busy day at work, I received a message from Allison, my college roommate. She didn't sound like herself and asked me to call her back. After I heard the message, I knew something was terribly wrong. I immediately called her and asked what was wrong with her dad. Allison was stunned! She asked, "How do you know that something is wrong with my dad?" I came clean and told her about my abilities. She confirmed that her father was in the hospital and that they didn't think he would make it through the night. I told her that he was going to be alright, and I heard that he is going home. But I should have clarified "which home" he was going too! He didn't make it that night. He went home to the Other Side. I learned a great lesson that day: Always remember to ask!

The following week I nervously walked into Sheila's class. I knew that I had to ask the students if I could read for them. So, a few minutes before class started, I asked my classmates if they would like me to read for them. If they did, I asked them to write their name on the sheet of paper that I passed around. To my surprise, everyone put their name down. I was very happy because I could complete my homework assignment.

I decided to read for one classmate each day. I would look down at the names on the last and chose one person to read for that day. Once I decided on the person, I would think of that person and then say their name out loud. After I did this, the evidence just started to flow in quickly for me. Most of the evidence that I received was through clairaudience or clairsentience.

The first person who I read for was Marissa. The evidence I received about her came quickly. I wrote it all down in an email. I had about eight pieces of evidence, which I shared with her. I checked my email to make sure it made sense and then I pushed the send button. I was so nervous, but I knew I had to trust what I received. Less than an hour later Marissa sent me back an email telling me I that I was spot on with my reading.

Here is the evidence that I gave her, and the Italics are her responses.

- I had told her that she was very sick because I felt this in my body. *Marissa said that she was battling cancer.*
- I told her that she needed to take it easy because her body was tired. *Marissa said that she had just gotten a radiation treatment, a week before.*
- I told her that she needed to buy a plant and put in her house. I also told her that the color "blue" was important. *Marissa said that she just bought a blue plant for her house.*
- I also told her that I felt she was sad. *Marissa said that she had gotten into an argument with her daughter which made her sad.*
- I told her that she needed to use her abilities more. *Marissa said that she was just starting to use them again because she had gotten so sick the year prior.*

I was amazed by the validations that I received. This helped me to build my confidence for the following my next readings.

I read for Christian next, and he also validated the evidence that I gave him.

Here is the evidence that I gave him. His responses are in italics.
- I told him that he needed to check his tires on his car. *Christian said that he had to get his tire fixed because it had a nail in it.*
- I told him that he was going to leave his job and move. *Christian said that he was leaving the United States because he was in the military. He would be moving the following month for his job.*
- I also felt that he was going to leave his relationship. *Christian said that he broke up with his girlfriend because of this move.*

Again, I was ecstatic that my reading was accurate for him! I continued to read for each classmate. In their responses, each classmate validated that the evidence I gave them was correct. I was thrilled about the success of my readings, and I couldn't wait to tell Jeanne.

I called her a few days later and told her about my homework. She was proud of me. She said that she knew that I could do this and that was why she pushed me so hard. I continued to work with Jeanne every other week for two more months straight. Then she told me that there wasn't anything left that she could teach me. Jeanne told me that I was ready to do it on my own!

She also told me that I needed to charge money for my readings too. Jeanne felt that I was now a professional reader. I still felt that I needed to practice more. I was sad that my training was done with Jeanne, but her guidance gave me confidence and propelled my abilities. Spirit knew I needed a mentor to guide me and that was exactly what Jeanne provided!

In April, I started to read Gordon Smith's *Intuitive Studies*. I immediately fell in love with this book. I couldn't put it down. Gordon is a well-renowned Medium in Scotland. In his book, he provides exercises at the end of the chapter to help you work on developing your abilities. Most of the exercises in the book require you to have a partner. I was disappointed by this, but I knew I would work on them soon.

I continued to attend Sheila's class, but I realized that the pace of it was now too slow for me. I had been on the fast track of spiritual learning while I was working with Jeanne and reading all these books. I did this because I wanted to grow quickly. I began to rethink Sheila's class. I called Kim and told her that I was going to quit the class. She told me that she felt the class was a bit slow for her too, but she was going to stick with it. Kim had studied under Sunny Dawn Johnson, a Medium in Phoenix. She took Sheila's class because she needed a refresher course. I told her that I hoped to see her in another class at Harmony.

After I spoke with Kim, I sent an email to Sheila to let her know that I was leaving her class. I thanked her for everything that she taught me and hoped to take another class from her. After I sent the email, I knew in my gut that this was right the decision for me. The next day I received a call from Kim. She decided that she was going to quit the class too. She said that she had thought about our conversation and felt that the class was too easy for her. This surprised me, but I understood why she felt this way. We both needed to leave that class in order to expand our skill sets in a more advanced class. It was a nudge from Spirit.

May rolled in, and Harmony offered a class called "Intuitive Studies." This class was based Gordon Smith's book! Spirit knew I wanted to work deeper with my abilities, and it fell right in my lap! I signed up immediately. I called Kim to let her know about the class. She wanted to take it too. We were excited to take another class together!

While we waited for the class to start, Kim asked me to have lunch with her. I agreed, and we met up a few days later. At that lunch, Kim asked me if I would like to start a spiritual business with her. She felt that my readings were strong, and she wanted to work with someone who wanted to help others too. Kim's business idea was to offer readings and healings to clients. While she was telling me this, I thought back to my reading with the woman in New Orleans. Her prediction was right!

Then my thoughts immediately switched to my job. How could I have a spiritual business and still do my job? I had been back in my job for year, and I loved it. It was my dream job, despite the any setbacks, and I didn't want to leave it again.

My mind filled with questions. Am I ready to charge clients' money for my readings? Will anyone want to pay me for a reading? What If someone from my job found out that I had a spiritual business giving readings? That would be the end of me in baseball! The questions kept reeling, but I listened to what Kim had to say. I told her that my job was very demanding, but I would think about it. I also thought that Kim was more accomplished at giving readings. I felt I needed more time to develop and practice. She told me to take some time to think it over and let her know what I decided. I left the restaurant not knowing what to do. But I knew in my gut that I had to really think about this.

I called Nikki, and she was thrilled at the idea. She had tried for years to get me to open some type of business. She told me to think about it but felt that I should try it and see. So, I heeded her advice. For the next several days I contemplated this opportunity. Whenever I thought about it, I felt that I needed to help Kim open this business. I thought that I could help her on the side. She could take all the readings and healings, and I would be backup if she needed me. I had this "urge" to call her and tell her I was in. I was going to be Kim's business partner. Kim was excited. She told me that we needed to work on a business plan. She also told me to start thinking about names for the business. We planned to have dinner in a few days to go over some of these details.

I arrived at the restaurant for dinner, it was packed. Kim was sitting at the bar because all the tables were taken. She told me there was no room to be seated but we could still order dinner. We decided on what we wanted and placed our orders. While we waited for our appetizers Kim asked me what I thought the name for our business should be. I told her that it should start with the word "chicks." Kim almost fell off her chair! She couldn't believe that I just said the word "chicks." She told me that she thought the name should be "Chicks with Spiritual Kicks." I liked it, but something was just a bit off. I thought about it for just a bit and told her it needs to be "Chicks with Spiritual Gifts" (CSG). She agreed and that was that. We had our business name! We started to work on the business plan that night, and for several weeks to come.

The Intuitive Studies class started while we were working on our business plan. I was excited to expand and learn more in this new class. The instructor's name was Keith. He was the pastor of the church and a jovial man who loved music. He had the chairs set up in a circle, just like in Sheila's class. I took a seat. When Kim arrived, she sat next to me. A girl named Christina sat on the opposite side of me. We started to talk. She was outgoing, cheerful and, friendly. As we spoke, more people arrived. Twelve people started that class.

I looked around and took notice of a few people that stood out to me. They were Christina, Lorina, Jody and Corinne and, of course, Kim. I was not sure why, but I felt my claircognizance kicking in. Over the several weeks of classes, the six of us became good friends. Each person offered something different to our group.

Lorina was clairvoyant, clairaudient, and clairsentient and worked as a hairdresser. She also worked as an energy healer on the side and loved working with crystals. Jody was clairvoyant and clairsentient and worked at an architect firm. She used to be a massage therapist but left the healing field because it drained her energy. Corinne was clairvoyant and clairsentient and worked as a middle school teacher. She loved books and writing. Christina was clairvoyant and clairsentient and worked as a nurse. Christina loved to journal and write. Kim was clairvoyant and clairsentient and worked as an acupuncturist. As for me I was clairaudient, clairsentient and claircognizant. I was the only one in the group that was not clairvoyant.

As we built our friendships, we created a tight bond, like a sisterhood of sorts. We loved to see each other in class but would meet outside of class too. When I told the group that Kim and I needed to find an artist to draw our business logo, Jody said that she worked as a graphic designer on side! She said that she would be happy to help us. We all just laughed because we knew that this was meant to be.

I told Kim that I would take care of designing the logo since I did this type of work with my job. She agreed to let me take the lead on this. The next day while working in one of the stores, I received a nudge from Spirit. An idea for the CSG logo flashed in my mind. I found a pencil and printed off some receipt paper from the register. I started to draw this logo that was in my mind. Less than five minutes later, the logo was complete. I took a picture of it on my phone and sent it over to Jody. She took a week to draw it out. Kim and I loved it. We had the official CSG logo for our business.

When the logo was completed, Kim quickly worked on our website. We became an online business a few weeks later. However, we needed to figure out how to take in-person clients. Kim decided to rent a space from our friend Zach who had an acupuncturist business. She was going to work on both acupuncture and CSG readings in this space. We decided that Kim was going to be the main person for CSG. I would help her on the side when she needed me. The business was officially up and running. We were excited for this new adventure.

Once the business up and running, Kim and I decided to take a Reiki workshop from Joy from my YAYA group. Reiki is a Japanese healing modality where you use your hands to clear energy. We felt that we could offer reiki as a healing service for our business. The workshop amazed us. Both Kim and I loved healing with our hands. We completed level one and then took level two. We earned our certificates and could now offer this service to our clients. The business was making baby steps, and I felt at peace. That peace was short lived. Spirit decided to give me another BIG nudge.

That summer, Keith informed us that two Mediums were coming to Harmony to teach a five-day Mediumship workshop. These men, Sandy and Dominic, were well known mediums in Scotland. The classes were going to be held at night and over the weekend. There was a limited number of seats for the workshop. If you wanted to attend, you needed to RSVP.

When Keith mentioned this, I didn't feel that I needed to take this workshop. Besides, my schedule at work was crazy because I was up against some major buying deadlines. I didn't have the time to take this workshop now. I talked to Kim about it. She wasn't going to take the workshop either because she was going out of town that week. This was the same for Corinne as she was going to visit her parents. Christina, Jody, and Lorina immediately signed up for the workshop. I knew that they would have a great time.

Teddy began nudging me to sign up for the workshop, but I didn't listen. He finally figured out a way for me to listen. A few days before the workshop, Keith called me at work. He had never called me before, so I thought that it was a bit strange. I found out quickly why Keith was calling me. There was one seat left for the Mediumship workshop. Keith had an "urge" to call me because he felt I needed to attend. He didn't want anyone else to reserve that seat because he felt it belonged to me. I knew that my guide Teddy had something to do with this, so I agreed to take the last spot.

I hung up the phone and thought, "What have I got myself into?" My mind was racing because I was currently taking work home at night to meet my buying deadlines. I wondered how I would fit the workshop into my schedule. I quickly realized that I would make it work. I also told Teddy, "Thanks for having Keith call me. I got the message!"

The workshop started a few days later. The girls were happy that I was taking the workshop with them. We all sat in the same row of seats, eager to learn new material. Sandy and Dominic introduced themselves, and we dove right into the Mediumship workshop. I learned so much about myself during those five days. I was giving accurate messages to other students that I had never met before. I was taken aback, because I didn't realize how easily it was for me to connect mediumistically. This workshop helped to propel my abilities. I began to understand how my abilities worked and how to give psychic and Mediumship messages in readings together. Not to mention I became great friends with Sandy too.

I called Nikki to share my experience with her. I told her what I learned and informed her that I was a Medium. She was excited for me and asked if I wanted to give more readings. I told her that I did. Then Nikki told me that she wanted me and Kim to come to Las Vegas in September. She wanted us to read at the 10th anniversary party for her business, a hair salon called NY Hair Company.

I told her that Kim will be fine because she has given readings before, but I wasn't sure if I was ready yet. Nikki disagreed. She told me that I was 100% ready. She trusted me with her clients and knew that I would give great readings too. Nikki was always supporting me! I relented and told her that we be would happy to offer readings and to celebrate her business. I called Kim to share the news. She was excited and we started to plan what we needed to bring to Las Vegas for the event. It was the Voice of Spirit.

While I was working on the business, I still was busy with my job. The season was getting ready to come to the end. I was at the ballpark helping in the store when I ran into Steve. He gave me a big hug and we talked a lot. I hadn't seen to him in a while, and he wanted to know how my job was going. I gave him the update on the job, but I didn't share the news about CSG with him. Steve didn't believe in spiritual things. He would consider it "woo woo." After we caught up, we talked about having lunch soon. After he left, I thanked Spirit for letting me see him again. At that time, I didn't realize that my statement to Spirit would become so powerful. I would learn this later down the road.

As the weeks went by, Kim was reading for more clients. If I was available, we would read clients together. This was a great experience for me because it helped me build more confidence with my readings. This became evident when it was time to read at Nikki's event.

Kim and I flew to Las Vegas and gave readings the entire day. We offered $10 readings for 10 minutes to coincide with Nikki's 10th anniversary theme. Some clients purchased several 10 minutes readings and combined them together to lengthen their overall reading. When we started the readings, Kim and I read together. Eventually, we had to read in separate rooms because there were so many clients waiting for their readings. Our readings were so popular that we read for about 50 people that day.

As I read, I noticed that many clients left crying. I knew that crying meant that they were healing emotional wounds. My readings were touching people's souls. At one point a man came into my room and asked me what I was doing to these people because everyone was coming out crying. He laughed and said that he was joking. He told me that he wanted me to help him too and requested a reading with me! After he left, I was surprised that people were noticing the clients were crying. I was a bit worried, but Nikki came to tell me that I was helping so many of her clients. She wanted me to know this and to keep up the good work. When the event ended, I was exhausted but grateful. Now I had the confidence that I needed to read clients by myself.

Kim and I started discussing how we could bring in more business for CSG. We reached out to our friend Tina who helped Kim build our website. Not only was she great with "tech stuff," she was also a marketing genius and knew social media like the back of her hand! Tina told us to write weekly blogs that would show our clients that we were experts in our field. This would also help with algorithms that would rank our business higher. The more that you post on the internet, the higher your business ranks when someone searches your topics. We decided that Kim would post on social media and continue to update the website while I would write blogs each week. We had our action plan!

While we were busy with CSG, the fall semester of the Intuitive Studies class was about to begin. Kim decided that she wasn't going to take another semester. She wanted to focus on our business. I decided that I wanted to take more classes with the girls. I saw them all for the first night of class and told them how the event went. They were excited for us! Many of them felt that CSG was going to become busier in the next month. And it did.

Kim was busy giving more readings to clients. However, as she gave more readings, her unhappiness increased. Kim wanted to do something different, but she didn't know how to tell me. The night before I left for a weeklong conference in Las Vegas, she called me and asked to meet her at a café. She wanted to discuss CSG. I knew something was "off" as I hung up the phone, but I didn't know what it was. I met up with her later that night, and she told me how she felt about our business.

The increasing number of readings helped Kim realize that this was not the work she wanted to do. She wanted to pursue healing with Earth medicines like Ayahuasca and Kambo. I listened to her speak and was in a stunned silence. I didn't realize that she was feeling this way! I collected my thoughts and told her that I respected her decision. I welcomed her to do more readings with me if she wanted. She was happy about the offer and relieved that I wasn't upset. We talked a bit more about the transition. I was sad that she felt this way, but I wanted the best for her. I was grateful that she had been honest with me and herself. We said our goodbyes and parted ways. I told her I would talk with her soon.

I left the restaurant feeling completely overwhelmed. Questions flooded my mind.

How was I going to run this business and work fulltime?

How would I work the website?

How could I handle posting on social media?

Did I still want to have this business by myself?

The questions raced through my mind. I immediately called Nikki to tell her what happened. She put me at ease and said that I could do this. She said that if she can run her own business, I could too! Nikki offered to help me with anything that I needed. I told her what I was worried about and shared all the questions I had.

I was mainly worried about the website and social media. That was an area I was not skilled in. Nikki informed me that I could hire someone to take care of it. It was that easy! Nikki encouraged me to continue with the business to see how I liked it on my own. She advised me to not overthink it. I would just need to schedule readings around my full-time job. She told me to "breath" and let it go. I was going to see her in a few days. We could discuss more then.

As I hung up the phone, I knew in my gut that Nikki was right. I could run this business like anything else I did. The Voice from Spirit was giving me another nudge. That was the moment I decided I was the owner of CSG, and it was now my business!

I flew to Las Vegas the following day. I put all my efforts into my job. I was there for a baseball conference and had to keep my mind on that. A few days after I arrived, Nikki met me at my hotel. We had dinner and discussed the action plan I needed for my business.

Nikki told me that she talked to Megan about the "tech stuff" for my business. Megan was one of Nikki's employees. She oversaw the website and social media for Nikki's business. Megan offered to work for me. She could work 10 hours a week for a few months, helping me get my website and social media presence up and running. This was the best news I could receive! I felt this was going to be the toughest part of the business for me.

We then talked about the location. I had to figure out where I would give in-person readings. I decided to talk to Zach about renting a space at his business. We also talked about my schedule and how to work around it to give readings. Once the action plan was complete, I felt like this would work. I knew what I needed to do and was going to give it a shot! I was so happy that Nikki was there to help me at this critical time. Not to mention that it happened right before I went to see her. I knew that this was the Voice of Spirit.

When I returned home, Kim and I met up to go over the website and social media. She taught me how to post on the website. Kim also gave me all the social media information so I could give it to Megan. The last thing Kim told me was that she talked to Zach and told him what was happening. Zach told her that I could rent space at his place! I was thrilled because everything was falling into place.

A few days later, I had a reading with Sandy, from Scotland. He was in town because he was teaching another class at Harmony. Sandy told me about my business and said that the person I was working with was not happy. She needed to leave, and this would be the best situation for both of us. He told me not to worry because the business was going to be successful. I was shocked. Sandy was not aware of anything that had happened with CSG. I was grateful that the Voice of Spirit was coming through Sandy to me. The following night I went to class and shared the CSG news with the girls. They were surprised but encouraged because they knew I could do it on my own.

We also discussed what to do about our class. The holiday season was starting, and this would be the last class of the semester. We would not be able to practice for a few months. I still wanted to practice, so I asked the girls if they would like to start a weekly development circle. Everyone said yes, but we didn't know where to meet. We finally decided that we would meet weekly at my house. With the development circle in place, everything just seemed to flow easily. Spirit was helping me get ready for the new chapter that was emerging. I was excited for what the New Year was going to bring.

CHAPTER 2- CSG MY BUSINESS
2015

When January began, I had more time to work on CSG. The next six weeks at my job would be slow, so I knew that I needed to take advantage of that time. I immediately started to put things in motion. I worked with Megan to increase the CSG social media exposure. We also worked on a monthly newsletter to send out to my clients too.

Once that was in place, I started to become more efficient on the CSG website. I reached out to Tina to make a few changes on the website. Then I called Zach to talk about renting a space. We decided that I would work around his schedule and read out of the lobby on Friday nights and all-day Sunday. This was the best plan of action because I didn't know how many in-person clients I would have. Plus, I had to continue to work around my job schedule, which to my limited time. But Spirit had a plan in mind for me, which would work out flawlessly.

A few weeks later I received a call from my boss James. He informed me that we lost the contract for the Arizona Diamondbacks, but I still had a job buying for the Washington Nationals. I was losing my office at the stadium where the Diamondbacks played, but I would be working from home. I was sad that I would not be buying for Diamondbacks. I had been buying for them for almost 10 years. However, I was grateful that I still had my job, and it gave me the opportunity to be able to work out of my house! Since I would not be working long hours at the ballpark, I would have more time to work on CSG. I could offer more readings. I knew that Spirit was helping me adjust to be the sole owner of CSG.

As I worked through my job transition, the Intuitive Studies class started again. Everyone took the class except for Kim. Our abilities were getting stronger, and it was noticeable. Keith even asked us if we would like to demonstrate our abilities on "platform" for the upcoming Sunday service. Platform is when a Medium works in front of an audience giving messages. I was nervous but knew this was the next step for me. I told Keith that I would demonstrate along with Christina and Corinne.

Sunday arrived, and I met the girls at Harmony. We all were nervous but encouraged each other. I talked to Christina and asked if she wanted to work together to read people. I would read them clairaudiently while she would read them clairvoyantly. She thought it was a great idea and agreed. We ran it by Keith, and he loved the idea too.

During the service, Keith called up me and Christina to give platform readings. I started by choosing the person to be read. I gave some evidence from a Loved One who had passed. Then Christina gave her evidence from that person too. For the next 10 minutes we went back and forth, building off each other's evidence. Our reading flowed easily, and the evidence coincided too. We went on to choose two more people for readings using the same process. Those readings were just as good as the first. We were both happy and relieved.

When it was Corinne's turn, she was able to easily read for two other people. Once it was over, we were thrilled that it turned out well. Keith was also overjoyed. After the service, he told us that we all gave great evidence for our readings and asked us to demonstrate again at a future service. We were ecstatic and agreed. Spirit was giving me another nudge to continue to work on platform.

In February, I was working at the NBA All-Star Game in New Orleans. It was an extremely busy week, but my co-workers and I had fun at night. We explored New Orleans and absorbed the nightlife. The night before I left, Patsy and I went to get tarot readings in St. Andrews Square. The woman who did my reading told me that I was still sad over my breakup with Daniel and I needed to move on. She also saw me having my own business too! I agreed with her on the sadness, but I didn't understand the business comment. I just let it go and left it at that!

Later that month, Alan, a vendor I worked with, came to town. He was a wonderful friend and wanted to catch up with me because we hadn't seen or talked to each other for some time. We met for dinner had a long overdue chat. I told him all about CSG and that I was a Medium. Alan was amazed and thought that it was wonderful.

While we talked, his mother, who had passed, came through and wanted to give him a message. I told Alan that his mother was here and that she wanted to give him a message. This is something that I normally don't do unless someone asks for a reading, but Alan was a friend, and I felt that I needed to tell him about this. I asked for his permission to relay the message from his mother. He agreed.

As I connected with his mother, she told me that she wanted Alan to know she was sorry. She gave me more evidence to share with him. She ended the message by telling me about a beautiful picture he had on his wall that reminded him of her. When I told Alan, his mouth dropped, and tears rolled down his face. He confirmed that his mother was hard on him because he chose to be an actor. His siblings were doctors and lawyers, and she gave him a hard time about it. So much so that he felt that she didn't love him.

Alan also validated the other evidence, including the huge picture on his wall. Once the reading was finished, Alan was in awe that I gave him so much evidence from her. He thanked me for the reading and told me that it really helped him. He confessed that recently, he had been having a hard time dealing with the loss of his mother. I told him that I was stunned too because I hadn't known that his mother had passed away. I felt blessed that I was able to help Alan out and give him the closure that he needed.

I started to read for more in-person clients weeks later. I also decided that I needed to offer phone readings. I added this service to the website and worked these around my job. Several clients booked phone readings, and my calendar filled up quickly. Between having a full-time job and running a business, I didn't have much time for myself. But I loved giving readings to my clients. I met some wonderful people, and I was grateful to help them.

Several clients told me that they wanted to learn how to use their abilities. I advised them to take classes at Harmony with Sheila and Keith. They were thrilled to have new people come to their classes. I didn't know why I was referring my clients to take classes, but Spirit had a new opportunity on the horizon for me.

In March, things were going great at my job and with my business. Then I received a call from Denise, the president of the board at Harmony. She told me that Keith had resigned and was no longer the pastor. Denise wanted me to tell his students. She felt the news would be best coming from me since most of his students were my clients. I agreed and told her I would meet her at Harmony later that night.

The evening, I informed the students about Keith. I let them know that they were in good hands with the other instructors at Harmony. Everyone took the news well, and I felt it would be a smooth transition. That feeling was short lived. As the week progressed several of the students decided that they didn't want take classes with anyone else. They loved Keith! Then Sheila decided to take a break from teaching the beginning Intuitive Studies class. It became a bit chaotic at the church.

Denise called me and asked if I would teach the last of Sheila's classes. I was shocked because I had not taught classes before. I knew the material but questioned whether I could teach it. However, I knew that it was the Voice of Spirit speaking through Denise. I agreed, but only if it worked around my schedule. I hung up with Denise and called the girls to tell them about my teaching opportunity. They were excited and cheered me on. With their support I felt that I could do it too!

The following weekend, I ran into Christina at Harmony, and we talked more about the upcoming Intuitive Studies class that I was going to teach. She encouraged and said she believed I could do it. As she got ready to leave, she asked me if I wanted to get my tarot cards read. Christina was going to an event that had tarot card readers and thought it might be good idea to find out how my new teaching opportunity would go. I agreed.

Christina had been to this store before, but it was new to me. I was assigned a tarot reader named Alisha. She laid out the tarot cards and began my reading. She immediately told that I was a teacher and that I would be teaching others. I asked her if I would enjoy teaching. She emphatically responded, "Yes!" After this she told me my business would become full-time. I validated that I did have a business and that it was just a part-time gig. She said that that would change within a year. I looked at her and was taken aback. I was thinking to myself "I am not ready to leave my full-time job yet because I need more clients to work full time." She must have seen my face and assured me that it would be full-time, and it would go well.

When we left, I told Christina what Alisha said about having a full-time business. Christina told me to tell Spirit how much time I needed for the transition. I immediately knew that she was right! I needed Spirit to know how much time I needed!

I told Spirit that I needed a year before I could transition out of my job. Even more specifically, I said that I needed more clients and confidence before I make this change. I ended the conversation by telling Spirit that I knew that you want me to do this work full time, I just need a bit more time to get to that place. When I finished talking to Spirit, I knew in my heart that I made a promise, and I had a year to do it!

I started teaching Intuitive Studies the next week. I already knew a few students in the class, so I introduced myself to the other students. The class was amazing! I realized that I loved teaching. Over the next few weeks a few students dropped out, but new students took their place. I realized that whoever I was supposed to teach would be in my class. I trusted Spirit to guide me through. And that is exactly what happened. The other classes I taught were amazing too, and Denise asked me to teach the class again the following semester. I agreed. After I taught the Intuitive Studies classes, I had to turn my attention back into my buying job because the busy season was starting. Up to this point, I had been able to handle my buying job and CSG with no problems, but that changed abruptly the following month.

With the arrival of May, I traveled for my job and caught up with some baseball friends. We always had a great time together, but I became concerned about a woman named Jules. Outwardly, she seemed to be having a good time, but I knew it was a façade. I could feel her energy. She was filled with sadness and anxiety. I pulled her aside and told her what I felt. She looked at me with surprise. She asked me how I knew this. I was nervous because I had not told anyone in our group about CSG or my abilities, but I took the leap and I told her that I was a Medium and had a side business giving readings.

I explained my abilities to her and said that was how I able to sense her energy. Jules looked at me stunned. She confessed that she believed in Mediums and had a spiritual side. Jules also validated that she was experiencing sadness and anxiety. She told me that she was not happy with her husband and was thinking of divorcing him. We discussed this, and I offered advice on what to do. I shared with her how I felt about him. I had felt in my gut that he was the right person for her, but I never told her. I realized now that my claircognizance was giving me the message. She just shook her head. Jules couldn't believe that I felt this way so many years ago. I asked her not to tell anyone about me being a Medium or having a business. I told her that I would tell everyone when I felt more comfortable explaining it. She agreed but asked me if I could tell her co-worker Renee. I agreed, and we left it at that.

The next morning, Renee pulled me aside to talk. She wanted to know more about me being a Medium. The conference was about to start, so I told her that we could talk later that night. She agreed.

Then I met up with my colleagues from the Nationals, Mary and her boss, Jeff. I had a great relationship with them. However, they were with a man I had not met. Mary introduced us. His name was Mark and had been recently hired by the Nationals to work on computer data. As soon as I met him, I knew something was not right. I felt his energy and didn't want to be around him. I brushed this feeling off and focused on the conference.

Later that night, I asked Mary about Mark. She said he was hired to analyze all the data on merchandise to make sure that it was turning and moving. She added me that things were going to change and that she was not sure what would happen. Mary said that the arrival of Mark and the unknown changes had caused to start looking for another job. As soon as I heard this, I knew that this wasn't going to be good.

I left Mary and met up with Renee. We discussed how my abilities worked and what a Medium does. Renee told me that she had never had a reading before and wanted to see how it worked. I gave her evidence about her grandmother who had come through. Renee was shocked and couldn't believe I was telling her about her grandmother and how she passed. Then her grandmother shared evidence about Renee's new son. Renee's grandmother said that he had almost fallen but that she had caught him and nothing bad happened. When I told Renee, she had tears in her eyes. She explained that her son had almost fell, but something stopped him from hitting the ground. Renee said that she couldn't explain it at that time, but now she understood why.

I gave Renee more evidence, but what I told her next shocked her. Her grandmother told me to tell Renee to stop eating McDonald's food. Renee burst out laughing! She told me that her biggest secret was eating McDonald's hamburgers and fries. Renee said it was a dirty little secret that no one knew, not even her husband. When I finished her reading, Rachel told me that she now believed in Mediums. She said that there was no way I could have known any of this evidence. She added that she would not tell anyone about me being a Medium until I was ready to divulge it to the others.

At the conference the following day, I worked with Mary and Mark. Again, I did not like Mark's energy and didn't want to be around him. He was very demanding and wanted things his way. Mark had never worked in sports before and didn't know the protocols of the business. He wouldn't listen to anything we had to say. Mary just looked at me and rolled her eyes.

Mary announced that she was leaving to work in her room on some business. She also informed me that she was going to leave the conference early. I knew that she was not speaking the truth. Mary always stayed until the end of the conferences. In my heart I believed that she wasn't going to put in any more effort to accommodate Mark because she was leaving her job soon. I understood why she left and didn't blame her. Unfortunately, I was left to work with him as best as I could.

After Mary left, Mark found me talking to my vendor Sam. Mark demanded that Sam produce a new graphic shirt and deliver it within two weeks. I just looked at him and felt like calling him an idiot. Sam looked at me. I could tell by the look on his face that he was thinking, "Are you kidding me?" We both knew that what he wanted could not be done within that timeframe. There were protocols and approvals that needed to be signed off on before a shirt becomes printed. The timeline to get a new design approved is about six weeks. Nevertheless, I just let him talk and let him believe that he could bulldoze his way into getting it done. Once he left, I profusely apologized to my Sam. I felt bad that he had to deal with the wrath of this new guy. Sam knew it wasn't me but told me that we were going to have a rough time with him. I agreed.

Later, I emailed my bosses and shared Mark's demands with them. Both immediately responded. They couldn't believe that he was demanding things already. Aaron agreed that what Mark wanted could not be done in that timeframe. The approval process would take six weeks or longer. James's email asked why I was unable to handle him and his requests. James knew I could make things happen with my vendors. He also knew that I got along with everyone, so I was sure my email surprised him.

I replied, telling that James that Mark was demanding and did not want to compromise on anything. I told him that it was Mark's way or the highway. He was the type of guy that would not be happy with anything, and he would expect you to jump through hoops. Aaron told James that he would deal with Mark. James was known for being demanding too, so it made sense that Aaron would pass Mark off to him. James replied, saying that he would take care of it. I thought to myself this would be an interesting matchup. I wondered who would win this battle!

After the email exchange, I had plans to meet Mark for dinner. I was not looking forward to spending any more time around this guy or his energy. I arrived at the restaurant to find Mark at the bar drinking heavily. I discovered that he liked whiskey and bourbon on the rocks. I shook my head because Spirit knew that the only thing that I could not handle was an alcoholic! My father was one, and I made sure I was not around this type of behavior. I looked at Mark and chuckled because Spirit was smart. Working with an alcoholic was my limit. Spirit knew this.

When Mark spoke, he slurred his words. And his eyes were bloodshot. I asked him how long he had been at the bar. Mark said that he had been there for over an hour. While he talked, Jules and Renee walked into the restaurant. They saw us and immediately walked over. I had told them earlier about Mark, so they knew about his energy. When they saw the state he was in, they looked at me and came up with an excuse for me to leave. I asked Mark if he knew how to get back to the hotel. He told me that he did, and we left. I was so grateful that the girls saved me. We couldn't believe how drunk he was, but we all gave him the benefit of the doubt as it might have been just a one-time experience.

At eight the next morning, I walked with Jules and Renee to the conference. I got there and saw Mark drinking bourbon on the rocks! Surprise, surprise! The girls and I looked at each. We just knew that he was an alcoholic. I made sure I sat with them during rest of the day because I couldn't be around Mark. Later, I sent an email to my bosses to let them know about Mark's drinking. I shared with them that I didn't sit with Mark because he had been drinking. After I sent the email, I knew in my gut that working with Mark was going to be a challenge. Little did I know that the challenge was right around the corner.

Mary gave her notice and left the job shortly after the conference. Jeff, her boss, was moved to a new department within the Nationals. I had to work with Mark exclusively, and it was a headache to say the least! Mark called me at all hours of the day demanding things. If he felt that I didn't get him what he wanted, he would than demand it from my boss James. Normally James was not a man to back down, but he wanted me to do whatever I could to make Mark happy. James now understood what kind of person Mark was. His requests became so unreasonable that I nicknamed him "Coco" to my friends. I said that he was "cuckoo" like the bird from Coco Puffs ® cereal. Nevertheless, I tried to accommodate his requests and get him what he wanted, but I couldn't take him or his energy. I asked Spirit to help me deal with him so I wouldn't be pushed over the edge.

Even though my job with Coco was stressful, CSG was joyous and my clientele was increasing. My readings were fun, and I felt that I was helping people. I knew this because I started to receive more referrals from my clients. I also had repeat clients too. Many of my clients told me how much I was able to help them in their lives, which in turn, made me feel joy. I knew I was making a difference, and I felt blessed. The more blessed I felt, the more clients I booked. It was the work of Spirit! Since my schedule was packed, I didn't have a lot of down time. I was grateful for my friends because they would work around my schedule to see me. They were my sounding board about Coco and my cheerleaders for my business. It truly was a blessing.

In June, I had to go on two buying trips with Mark (Coco). I dreaded these trips because I was going to be alone with him. First, I flew to Kansas to meet up with him. When I got off the plane, I couldn't find Coco. I looked around but he wasn't anywhere to be found. I located our driver who told me that he was in the bathroom. We waited about 10 minutes, then I saw him walking to the car. He reeked of alcohol. I asked him how many drinks he had on the plane. He slurred his words and said only a few. "A few too many!" I thought to myself. Then he said, "I don't know why I like you, but I do for some reason." I wanted to laugh because I knew that it was Spirit's doing!

Our vendor, Amy, picked us up the next morning so we could start our buying meeting. Coco was not interested in the buying. He worked on his computer the entire time. It came across as quite rude. I felt bad for Amy. I'm she wondered why he came in the first place. After the trip, I reported what happened to James.

The following week I met Coco in Boston for our second buying trip. Joey, our vendor, picked us up for dinner along with another baseball team. At dinner, Coco became intoxicated and said some very inappropriate things. Joey, who is a very laid-back man and can handle these things, was completely stunned. He just looked at me and shook his head. He knew that Coco had too much to drink. Joey tried to end the evening. He said that it was getting late and we had an early morning meeting. Coco argued with him. He wanted to go out and see the town. So, Joey humored him. He agreed to have one last drink at the bar next door. This appeased Coco for the moment.

As we walked outside, Coco received a phone call and walked away. During his absence, I profusely apologized to Joey and the other baseball team. They told me to stop because his behavior had nothing to do with me. They said they felt bad because I had to work with him. As we talked, 10 minutes passed. Then another 10 minutes passed. Joey was fed up and said that he was going to just go get him. Just as Joey went to get Coco, a car drove up, Coco got in, and the car drove away. We were stunned because he didn't know anyone in Boston. Joey tried calling him on his phone, but there was no answer. We figured he must have ordered an Uber and drove to the hotel. He was so drunk that he probably forgot that we were waiting for him!

As we drove back to the hotel, Joey told me that Coco's behavior had been inappropriate and that he would not be invite him back for another buying trip. I agreed with him and gave him my apologies. When I got back to the hotel, I checked to see if Coco was there. He was not. I was concerned, but there was nothing I could do. An hour later Joey texted me and said me that he heard from Coco. He was back in the hotel. I was grateful to hear this news because at least I knew that he was okay.

When I saw Coco the next morning, he acted like nothing had happened. And he didn't apologize to Joey when he picked us up! I was shocked. Then we arrived at the office to start our buying day. As Joey started to show us the buying line, Coco opened his laptop. I thought he was going to take notes, but he started to watch live sports on his computer. I was floored. He didn't pay attention to Joey's buying presentation at all! Joey called Coco out for his behavior. Coco just replied, "Terri oversees all the buying. I don't need to listen, she does!" Joey and I looked at each other. I knew what he was thinking, "Then why are you here?" Joey pulled me aside at the end of the day and told me that he was going to speak to my bosses about Coco. I told him that I understood. Joey's company had paid for Coco to come on this buying trip.

As Joey drove us to the airport, I was grateful that the nightmare trip was over. While I waited for my plane to board, I sent an email to my bosses to tell them know about Coco's behavior. I needed to alert them because Joey was going to contact them to give them the details. I knew Joey well enough to know that would not hold back his true feelings! My bosses were going to get an earful from him, and I knew it wasn't going to be pretty!

The next day, James called me. He said that Joey had called him. He went on to say that he was sorry that I had to be around Coco's behavior. Unfortunately, there was nothing that he could do about it because he didn't want to "rock the boat" with Coco's boss. Plus, Coco didn't work for our company, so James's hands were tied. He knew that Coco's behavior reflected poorly on our company and was negatively affecting our vendor relationships.

James then told me something interesting. Prior to the buying trip, Coco told him that he wanted me to live in Washington, D.C., because he wanted a buyer on site! James informed him that I would not move. The best compromise involved me traveling there once a month. I agreed with James and told him that I would coordinate my schedule to appease Coco. After I hung up the phone, I knew that this was going to be another challenge.

I was going to have to juggle more travel in addition to my CSG work. I was nervous, but I shrugged it off because the season was ending in three months. I also asked Spirit daily to help me with Coco. I asked Spirit to do whatever you feel is the best for him so we wouldn't have to work together anymore! The requests worked. When I arrived in D.C. a week later, I never saw Coco. He said that he was too busy to see me. I knew in my gut that he was not going to meet me, he just wanted to demand things. It was part of Spirit's plan for me not to have to interact with him. My prayers had been answered!

As July rolled in, I was still busy with the buying job and CSG. Spirit helped me balance them both. One of my vendor's, Farrah, told me that she would come to Phoenix to show me the new spring line. Farrah knew how difficult Coco was, and she was happy to work with me in Phoenix. We had a great time, and I picked out the items for the following season. After wrapping up the work, we started talking about spiritual things. I told Farrah about CSG. She was amazed. I gave her a reading from her grandmother. She was overjoyed and was completely shocked when I told her that her grandmother wanted her to make her bed. She looked at me and laughed. Farrah told me that before she came to see me, she was running late didn't have time to make her bed. Her grandmother had been a very tidy lady who believed making your bed was something you had to do. Farrah couldn't believe that her grandmother was acknowledging this. Farrah left happy with this message and the validation that grandmother was around her.

Nikki came to visit me shortly after Farrah left. She needed to talk. Nikki was trying to decide if she wanted to have a baby. She'd been thinking about this for years, but she needed to decide soon. Her doctor recently told that she didn't have too much time left to become pregnant. As we talked, I asked her to close her eyes. Nikki is clairvoyant, so I talked her through seeing different pictures in her mind. I asked if she saw a baby within her mind's eye, or if she saw a picture. She told me that the picture she saw was her on the beach with a baby boy about two years old. The baby had sandy blonde hair with some waviness in it. I asked her if she felt that this was her baby and she said, "Yes." When she opened her eyes. I reminded her of what I told her two-year prior. I told her that a baby boy would come to her if she wanted one. Nikki just looked at me and her eyes became wide. She had forgotten that I told her that!

I explained that if she really wanted to have a baby, then she needed to work on manifesting this baby in. I told her that she needed to be 100% sure that she wanted the baby. She also had to make sure her husband was 100% on board. Only then would Spirit give her one. Nikki decided that she really wanted to have a baby and was going to do what I suggested. I was happy that I was able to help her and knew that this baby would be coming soon.

As the following months went by the baseball season came to an end. I honored Coco's request and flew out to D.C. every month. But I never saw him. This did not upset me in the least! I was happy that I didn't have to deal with him, and I knew it was the work of Spirit.

Since the season wrapped up, I was able to focus more time on CSG. I was seeing more clients each month. I was also receiving more referrals from clients, which was a blessing. One referral came from a lady that owned an old fashion soda fountain restaurant and antique shop. She wanted me to come to her business to see if I experienced anything paranormal. I had never done this before, so I asked the girls and Kim to help. We were excited to find out what we would uncover.

A few days later, we met the owner and her daughter after the restaurant closed. We decided to walk around the place separately to find out what we received. We didn't want to taint each other's evidence so we could validate the experiences. We walked around the restaurant for almost an hour picking up evidence as we went. Once we finished, we met in a group and gave our findings to the owner and her daughter. Everyone was able to share what they experienced. Several of us had the same or similar evidence. Once everyone shared their evidence the owner gave us validation. My evidence included:
- A sad woman was attached to the soda fountain area. She would walk up and down the aisle of the restaurant and the lights would flicker. *The owner told me that the original owner of the restaurant had been heartbroken when her husband left her for a younger woman.*

- There was a boy with blue eyes who died from the drugs that were kept in the restaurant. *The owner said that the woman was sad because her only son with blue eyes died from a drug overdose from the drugs kept in the pharmacy.*
- I felt that there should have been a door where a wall was. *The owner said that there was a pharmacy in the back of the soda fountain shop where I felt there should have been a door.*
- A sat man in the back of the corner of the restaurant. *The owner said that there was a man patron that would come in daily and sit in the back-corner area.*
- A man near the bathroom couldn't speak. *The owner said that there was a male patron who lived across the street. He came in daily, who couldn't speak.*
- I also felt many other things in the different rooms due to all the antiques.

We all had similar findings, and the owner was amazed at the evidence we provided. She offered us pie and ice cream to thank us. We were all thrilled that we were able to help her and give her the validation of her restaurant. The following day I thought about the evidence that I received from the restaurant. I knew that I was my skill set was getting stronger and that my life would be changing soon. I realized I would soon be leaving baseball to work on CSG full time. I had mixed feelings about this. I loved my baseball family and thought that maybe, I could continue to do both for another baseball season. However, I should have known because Spirit was always one step ahead of me.

I attended another baseball conference in November. I was grateful that I didn't have to worry about Coco. Both Aaron and James were coming to personally deal with him. I would be able to see my baseball friends and not worry about accommodating Coco. At one point, James pulled me aside to talk. He said that he would be the direct contact for Coco. James would coordinate with me on what had to be done. I wanted to jump and down and celebrate! I was so grateful because Spirit heard my pleas. After speaking to James, I left and found my friends to share the good news. They were happy that I didn't have to directly deal with Coco anymore. We went on to enjoy the evening. I was on cloud nine because I was able to work on my buying plan without any of Coco's distractions which was a huge blessing.

The day before the conference ended, Jules and I walked to St. Andrews square so I could get a tarot card reading. The woman who read my cards told me that my business would become full time, and I would travel overseas for it too! I knew in my gut that this would happen. I thanked her for the reading, and we left. A nudge from Spirit.

Later that evening I decided to have dinner at the hotel with my two of my friends, Scott and Laura. We just wanted a quiet evening at the hotel. At the restaurant, I sat next to Laura and Scott was directly across the table from me. While waiting for our food, a Loved One for Scott came through. It was his grandfather. I brushed it off because I had not let Scott or Laura know about my abilities nor CSG. However, Scott's grandfather was so persistent that I had to share my secret.

I somehow got up the courage to tell them that I was a Medium. I explained that I had a business on the side helping people by giving readings to them. Laura was excited because she said that she believed in Mediums. Scott was skeptical. He said he didn't believe in Mediums and didn't want a message. Scott told me that if I gave him a message then he was going to leave the table. I told Scott that his grandfather really wanted to give him a message. Scott got up from the table and at that very moment, his grandfather told me to tell him to "sit down and listen." I told Scott exactly what his grandfather said. I had known Scott for years, and he knew I would never speak to him this way.

Scott reluctantly sat down and looked at me with his arms crossed. I knew that he was trying to be respectful, not only to me but also to his grandfather because manners had been very important to him. I reassured Scott that I would just pass on the evidence that his grandfather wanted to share. I gave him a message about his brother. As I kept giving him more and more evidence, Scott's eyes just kept getting bigger and bigger. He couldn't believe the evidence that I was sharing with him. He started to relax and uncrossed his arms. He really listened to the message I was giving him. Also, I could also tell that he wanting to cry but was holding the tears back.

I was grateful when the message ended because I was so cold. Lisa shared that she was cold too. We were cold because Scott's grandfather was standing in between our chairs. Scott didn't know what to think. He had a look of disbelief on his face, and I could see the wheels were turning in his head. When he finally spoke, he told me that he didn't believe in "this type of stuff" but knew me well enough to know that I couldn't make this up. There was no way I know any of this evidence I shared. Scott said that he was grateful that I gave him a message and that at least I was a "good witch." We all laughed. I was so grateful that Scott was open to the message and listened to it! After the reading we all called it a night and left to our rooms.

The following day Scott sat next to me at the conference. He said that he had immediately called his wife when he returned to his room to tell her about the message. After talking to his wife and contemplating what I had told him, he was able to validate most of the evidence. Nonetheless, he was stilled stunned about how it all happened. I told him to check on the rest of the evidence with his family and to let me know.

Scott called me a week and a half later to share some news. His aunt unexpectedly visited him and his family for Thanksgiving. He shared the evidence with her, and she just cried. His grandfather was her father and she was able to validate the evidence that he didn't know. Scott was blown away because he hadn't seen this aunt in several years. He said that her visit came from out of the blue. I told him that it was his grandfather's way of sharing the message with her. Scott agreed and was grateful that I made him stay to listen to his grandfather's message.

Scott also told me that Laura wanted a reading too. He said that she kept talking nonstop about his. I told him I would reach out to her. I read for Laura a few days later, and her grandmother came through. It was her favorite grandmother, and she gave her a wonderful message. She ended it by saying, "Remember my recipes." Laura cried hysterically because she had been going through the recipes and making her grandmother's favorites for the holidays. I was so happy that I was able to share that wonderful message with her.

Soon after, another vendor I worked with, Emily, posted about the anniversary of her dad's passing on Facebook. I sent her a note about CSG, telling her that I was a Medium. I told her that I would be happy to read for her if she wanted. She was ecstatic. I read for her the following day. Her father came through to give her and her mom a wonderful message. Emily wanted to know if her father was around. He shared that her mom had broken a dish and was very upset over it. Emily laughed because her mom had recently broken her favorite dish and was upset. He also talked about Emily's dogs. One was sick, and she was worried. Emily acknowledged this and told me that one dog was old and sick. She was worried it was going to pass soon. Her dad told her not to worry because that the dog would make it. And it did. Emily was overjoyed to hear from her dad and thanked me profusely. She was so happy that he was doing well, and he was watching over them. I was grateful that I was able to share that message with Emily.

When I woke up the next morning, tears were running down my face. I had had a terrible dream. This was unusual because I don't remember my dreams. It scared me. I dreamt that my dad, Steve, was telling me about his will. It was alarming. I didn't understand it, and it worried me. I wasn't sure why I was dreaming about my dad. I thought that the reading I did for Emily and her dad had carried over into my dream. I asked the angels to watch over him and protect him. It was the Voice of Spirit starting to prepare me for a future event that would rock my world

CHAPTER 3- CSG A FULLTIME BUSINESS
2016

After the holidays, I heard that the store in D.C. was closed. I thought that was odd because we had just been open for the holidays! I contacted James to find out what was happening. He said that he didn't know why the team closed the store, but he would get back to me. I knew in my gut that something was not right. Spirit was giving me a nudge.

James called me the next day to tell me that the Nationals had revoked our contract, and we would no longer be buying their merchandise. They were going to buy it internally. I was shocked but knew that Coco had something to do with it. James wasn't sure that he had a job for me but would check on things and let me know the following day. I immediately called Nikki and told her. She gave me some great advice. She said that I should stop putting energy into "that job" and to start working on "your business." Nikki advised me to offer some specials for CSG and put all my effort into that now. I took her advice and offered a Love special for the month of February.

I called some of my baseball friends to tell them the news. Jules reminded me of the tarot card reading from the woman in New Orleans. The prediction of having a full-time business the woman's prediction was right! Then Jules gave me some great advice too. She told me to try my business full-time for six months. If it didn't work out, then I should start looking for another buying job. What she said just felt right. It was my claircognizance kicking in. I knew that I had to give CSG a shot. I spoke with Spirit. I told them that I was going to give it six months. I said that if you want me to do this work, I will have to have continual clients at CSG to keep me busy. Then I told Spirit how many clients I needed to make ends meet. After this, I let go and tried not to worry.

James called the next day. He told me that he didn't have a job for me and wished me well. I thanked him for giving me the opportunity to work for Gameday Merchandising again. I was a bit tearful as I hung up the phone because my baseball job was officially over. I told Spirit I am working full-time for you now, and I need everyone up there to be my teammates. Then I contacted Nikki and my baseball friends to tell them it was official.

A few hours later, I started to switch my gears. I worked on changing my thoughts from baseball and putting my efforts into CSG. I noticed that the Love Reading Special that I emailed had traction. Several clients booked sessions, which made me happy. I worked on more specials for the year and wrote blogs. I also asked Spirit to guide me through this process and to make it an easy transition for me.

A few weeks later, Nikki called me to share some good news. She was pregnant and ecstatic about it. Nikki told me that she had kept asking God to help her get pregnant so she could be a mother. I was so happy that she took my advice and manifested this baby in. She told me that she was a high-risk pregnancy because of her age. I told her not to worry about this, just keep asking Spirit for help. After I hung up with her, I thanked Spirit for helping Nikki conceive this baby.

In February, I was busy giving readings. I had over 40 clients request appointments for the Love Reading Special that I offered. I also taught more classes at Rising Phoenix (aka "Harmony") which I enjoyed too. Spirit was making the transition to running CSG full-time business easier, and I was overjoyed.

The weeks turned into months, and my schedule was booked. Spirit made sure I made my quota each month. I tracked how many clients I read for at the end of the month. It was just a bit over the number I needed. Even though I was running a business, the sales were always secondary. I told Spirit that I wanted to help as many people as I could and to bring me anyone that needed my service. I trusted that Spirit would bring me the clients and I would serve them. I never advertised for my business. I was getting clients through referrals, reviews, or Spirit bringing them to me. I was proud of this because I trusted Spirit enough to help me make CSG, a success.

When June arrived, I realized I had been in business—successfully—for six months. I couldn't believe it and was just amazed. I thanked Spirit for helping me make CSG as a full-time business. Not only did I love helping clients, I also had freedom. I didn't have to worry about my schedule, trying to balance everything to make it work because I had been so busy traveling and working late nights and weekends at the ballpark. Now, it felt strange to be home some days and nights.

I still worked long hours for CSG, but I loved it because it was my business and I was making a difference. So many clients told me my readings changed their lives. Hearing these words made me feel blessed. I was helping clients one by one. I felt overjoyed to be able to have the opportunity to serve others.

I decided to celebrate the six-month mark with Nikki. I flew to Las Vegas, and then we drove to California. Nikki was due to give birth in a few months, and her belly was huge. When we arrived in California, she was exhausted and had to rest. She napped, then we went to eat and see the sunset. We talked about the many blessings that we had that year, including the baby and CSG.

Nikki earlier found that she was having a boy. She decided to name him after our Uncle Nick but was unsure of how she would spell it. I told her that no matter the spelling, I was going to nickname him "Niko." After discussing baby Niko, we talked about CSG. Nikki told me she was proud that I made my a business success. We discussed the freedom that owning your own business provides. This includes time, decisions, money and the hours that you work. Plus, we were able to help others, which made us feel good inside. We continued talking on the way back to our hotel. I couldn't help but feel filled with joy and happiness. Spirit had been trying to get me on this road for years. Finally, I was moving forward.

After the California trip, I received a call from a T.V. producer. She asked me to work on an episode of her show, "Unprotected," in Phoenix. It was a reality T.V. show, and the episode was going to bring a Medium and a ghost-hunting team together to help a family who had been experiencing paranormal activity in their home. They wanted to find out what was what was happening. The producer wanted the episode to focus on where there was anything or anyone in the house. I was a bit skeptical but finally agreed. A few days later, I met the producer Janelle. She introduced me to Jay and Marie, a well-known ghost-hunting team from Phoenix. We were going to work together in the episode.

The cameras rolled as we entered the house. We met the family, and they explained their experiences. As they spoke, a grandmother stepped in and gave me a message. This grandmother was from the wife's side of the family and shared some evidence about the family. I relayed that information to them. I was also told of a woman who had the first initial of an "L." It turned out to be the grandfather's wife. Everyone looked at me in disbelief. While I was relayed the messages, the gadgets from the ghost hunting team kept going off. They confirmed on their devices that something paranormal was happening. They sensed the temperature in the room dropped.

We continued to film. When Marie and I went up to the daughter's bedroom, it became very cold. Then Marie's gadgets started to go off again. The grandmother shared evidence about her granddaughter. I shared the message with granddaughter. It left her stunned. She became uneasy and asked if she could leave the room. When she left, the grandmother left too. After this, I sat down with the grandfather. His mother came through. As I gave him the message, tears streamed down his face. It was a message that he needed to hear. While I gave messages to the grandfather, Jay and Marie's gadgets picked up on his mother's presence too.

When we finished investigating, I told the family that it was the grandmother that was coming to the home. She was making her presence known and wanted to let them know that she was around. They were relieved that it was her. I left there happy because I was able to give some messages and validation to the family. I was also glad that I took the opportunity and gave it a chance. It was the Voice of Spirit.

In August, Nikki told me that she needed to have a C-section because her pregnancy was high-risk. She asked me to determine which day would be best for Niko's delivery. Nikki knew that I understood numerology, the study of numbers and the values that are associated with them. She told me which days were available, and I immediately choose one. I choose my grandfather's birthday. Nikki had completely forgotten it was that day. Even though the day held deep personal meaning, I still worked on the numerology of the days and provided Nikki with that information. She decided to give birth on our grandfather's birthday!

Niko was born on Oct 7 and was a very happy baby. Nikki was so overjoyed with him and that made me happy. Nikki traveled to Phoenix three weeks later, and I was able to finally see him. When I held him, he immediately took to me! I knew that we had known each other in another lifetime. If he was crying, he would stop immediately when I held him. This amazed Nikki. I told her that he could feel my energy and that it made him feel better.

As he grew, he loved to come to my house to see all the crystals and lights. I knew immediately that a combination of a Rainbow and Crystal child. These children are very gentle, sweet, and loving. They help others and love crystals. He also loved to play my Native American drum. We would drum constantly. I thanked Spirit because I was so blessed to have this child in my life.

In November, I finally had the chance to talk to Kim about her trip. She had just returned from Washington where she was certified as a Kambo practitioner. Kambo is a process that uses the secretion of the green leaf monkey frog found in the Amazon. The frog's poison is applied to "gates," or tiny openings, on a person's skin. The poison travels through the body, looking for anything that needs to be cleaned. Things that can be cleaned include anger, trauma, addictions, anxiety, PTSD, depression, etc. The poison finds these areas and rips them out. A person purges, which releases anything negative. I immediately knew that I had to have a session. I wanted to release any leftover childhood trauma from my childhood.

I talked to Lorina about Kambo, and she wanted to experience it too. A week later, we both had a few sessions of Kambo over a period of a few days. After the sessions, I realized how much pain from my childhood that I had held onto. As I purged, Kim shared the details of what I was releasing. Since she is clairvoyant, she can see the pictures of what someone has endured. Kim can then share what she sees and what emotions are released. Not only did I release past pain, I deepened my Mediumship skill set and became more intuitive. I now had a much clearer connection to Spirit.

A week later, I received a text from Jody, who I worked with at McKale, in December. She shared an article about Steve. It said that he had passed of cancer! I was blown away and cried hysterically. I didn't even know that he was sick. I couldn't believe that he didn't tell me. I had just recently texted him to wish him a happy birthday. He just replied, "Thank you." That was not a normal text from him, but I figured that he was busy with work. I thought we would catch up at Christmas. Unfortunately, I lost that chance. I reached out to the boys to give them my condolences. I also called Denise and told her the news. I was supposed to teach class that night but canceled my class. I was just too overwhelmed with grief. Steve was like a father to me. He was the person that I could always count on to be there. I couldn't believe that I didn't know that he had passed.

I went to his memorial service with my friend Val. As we entered the church, I noticed the many people who were there. I had the chance to catch up to the boys. Then we took our seats. I just watched as more and more people arrived. They had to bring out more chairs because there were so many people. I also saw Carrie from a distance. I didn't want to approach her. I still didn't understand why she had been so angry, but I knew that she had not gotten past it because she didn't let me know that Steve was sick. This was not the time to talk to her. I didn't want to make her any more upset.

During the memorial, people shared stories about Steve. I knew many of the stories but heard a few new ones too. Pictures of Steve showing him at different ages provided the background. I remembered many of them and wished I had more time to spend with him. He was only 61 when he passed. I just couldn't believe it. Grief made the next few weeks very tough for me. I couldn't even celebrate Christmas with Nikki because I was so sad. But leave it to Nikki to figure out the one thing that would cheer me up. She asked if I would be Niko's godmother. This made me so happy, and I agreed.

2017

Niko was baptized in the beginning of January. Our Uncle Nicko traveled from Greece to attend. We had a great time catching up, and I was able to put my sadness aside for a bit. After we dropped Uncle Nicko off at the airport, I drove with Nikki and the baby to Las Vegas to clear my mind. This was helpful because I was still so sad about Steve's passing.

When I returned, I looked for another distraction. I put all my efforts into an online class from Morris Pratt. Several people from Rising Phoenix were taking the class. It focused on the study of Modern Spiritualism. It covered psychic abilities, Mediumship, and religion, in 30 classes. I dove into the studies, trying to work on a class a night. I would read the material one night, then answer questions or write papers the following night. The schedule was grueling, but it took my mind off my grief. I finished all the classes a month and a half later and to submit my course work via mail.

Soon after, I received a call from the woman who was grading my homework. She told me that she was concerned with my first lesson and that it usually takes students over a year to complete all the course work. What she said shocked me. I told her that I had completed a master's degree and could handle the course work. I informed her of Steve's passing and that I was taking the classes to forget about my grief. She gave me her condolences and said she understood why I worked on the classes so quickly. I told her that I would resubmit the first homework assignment. I then asked her to check the next few. If she felt that they were poor, I would redo all the homework and resubmit it to her.

I hung up the phone and revisited my answers. I could understand why she was concerned. I hadn't answered some of the questions to my fullest potential. I knew grief played a part in this, so I went through, fixed my answers, and resubmitted my work. She called back a week later and said that she was impressed with my work. She said that she would grade the rest of my homework and get back to me.

A month later, I was notified that I had passed all the classes except for one. I was only two points shy of passing that class. She let me resubmit the answers, and I passed. I was elated that I completed and passed 30 classes in just two months. The class also took my mind off my loss, and for that I was grateful too. Now that I had passed the course, Denise at Rising Phoenix wanted to ordain me as a minister. Leslie, a friend who was also an associate minister, ordained me in front of several of my friends and students a few weeks later. I was thrilled by this because I had not anticipated becoming an ordained minister. It was a nudge from Spirit.

I began holding services for Rising Phoenix when my busy schedule allowed. It was at this time I had to move out of Zach's business because the building had been sold. Denise was very kind and allowed me to give readings at the church. I was grateful for the quick fix but knew that I would need a more permanent solution.

In April, Denise and I flew to Maryland to taking some weekend classes with the International Spiritual Federation (ISF). We both wanted to work on our Mediumship skill sets. There, we met Robin, the ISF president of the ISF, and Richard, the vice president. I was excited to finally meet Robin. The year before, he had been slated to teach at Rising Phoenix but got the flu and had to cancel the trip. We talked for a while, and he told me that the ISF holds classes one week a year, around the world. This August, the class would take place in Scotland. I expressed my interest and told him I would sign up. Denise wanted to go too, so we both signed up to attend the conference. We didn't work with Robin that weekend, but we enjoyed our time with Richard. He was great at pushing us to maximize our Mediumship skill sets. I learned a lot that weekend and was excited for the learning opportunity in Scotland that was just a few months away. The prediction the woman in New Orleans made was coming to pass. A nudge from Spirit.

Later that week I talked to Jody about the ISF and she signed up for the classes too. She also wanted to travel to Ireland. We told Denise, and she loved the idea. She decided to bring her daughter to travel with us. We were so excited for this girl's trip. Jody planned the trip for all of us. This was a great help for me because I was so busy with CSG. I continued to work out of Rising Phoenix, giving readings to my clients. I decided I would look for a permanent place after I visited Scotland.

The weeks flew by. Before I knew it, it was time for us to leave. Jody and I left before Denise and her daughter. We explored Ireland for a few days and then flew to Edinburgh in Scotland. I loved Edinburgh so much that I wanted to spend more time there. After visiting Edinburgh, we went on to St. Andrews, which was where the conference was being held. We spent a wonderful week meeting others, enjoying the classes, and exploring St. Andrews. When the conference ended, the girls split up to explore on their own. I went on to see Sandy in Dundee, Scotland, and taught a few classes at his center. It was great to see him and catch up. I later met up with Denise and her daughter. We flew back to the United States a few days later.

A month after returning from Scotland, I went to get my yearly mammogram. The doctor called me the next day to tell me she saw something on image. I was going to visit Nikki in Las Vegas for a few days, so I scheduled the follow up appointment for two weeks later. I couldn't believe this news! I didn't want to tell everyone. I felt it was best to keep it to a few people. I told Nikki, and she told me not to worry. Next, I called Lorina. She came over and clairvoyantly saw a mass stuck in the middle of my chest, so she performed some "energy healing" on me. When I told Lisa, she clairvoyantly saw the mass too and made me some tea to drink. The tea was made with herbs that her guides directed her to use. This would help to move this mass of energy in my body.

I asked Spirit to help clear this mass and release it from my body. I tried not to think about it and was grateful that I was going to be seeing Nikki. We had our annual canoe trip, which was also relaxing time. It was just me and Nikki on this trip, and that made me happy. I was able to rest and be in nature and continued to ask for help from Spirit. I continued to drink the tea that Lisa made for me.

The following week I went to the follow up appointment, where the technician took more X-rays. I waited for over an hour to hear something. I was called back to get an exam from the technician. The technician scanned different parts of my breasts, and then went to get the doctor. They both seemed perplexed when scanning my breasts. I asked them what was wrong. The doctor said that they could not find the mass on the new X-rays and couldn't see or feel any mass in my body. I asked her if I could see the X-rays. She agreed.

I looked at the before and after X-rays. There was a large mass on the first X-rays. The doctor profusely apologized, saying that it might have been the angle that it was taken. I told her that she didn't need to apologize because I was happy. I knew in my gut that Spirit had helped me move that mass out of my body. I didn't tell the doctor how I had moved the mass out of my body. I didn't think she would understand my holistic approach to healing. But I didn't care how it left, I was just happy it was not in my body any longer! As I left, I thanked Spirit for helping me release the mass. I told Nikki, Lorina, and Lisa the great news. Everyone was thrilled and happy that Spirit took it away, and I finally could let it go too!

October arrived, and I started to look for a permanent place my business. It took several weeks, but with the help of Spirit, I was able to find one. The place was not available until the middle to end of January 2018 because there were some renovations that needed to be performed before I could move in. Again, I asked Spirit to help me find a temporary place to work out of because I Rising Phoenix was no longer available. Spirit helped me find a temporary building, and I moved in. I was so happy that things were falling into place.

Soon after I found my short-term business rental, my friend Jakki called me to share her good news. She was going on a group tour to Egypt at the end of January. This was interesting to me. I had wanted to visit Egypt since I was a child. So, Jakki emailed me all the trip details. The trip looked like it was going to be fantastic. I didn't know if I could commit because the trip started at the end of January, around the same time I was to move into my new business space. I knew I had to let this go, and I asked Spirit to help me. I asked that my new business space would be ready before the Egypt trip. I asked daily and trusted the process. I set the cutoff date to be the beginning of December because I would have to decide if I was going to take the trip.

Jakki and I spoke several times. I told her that I was trusting Spirit to help guide me on this decision. One night soon after, I woke up in the middle of the night and had the urge to sign up for the Egypt trip. I immediately signed up and paid the deposit. I then called Jakki to tell her that I was going. She was elated because I would also be her roommate during the trip. I hung up and asked Spirit to make sure that I could move into the new business space before I left for Egypt. I also needed to be in the space so I could teach my spring classes. I was taking a gamble, but I trusted that Spirit would make it happen. I continued to ask Spirit daily to make everything work out and knew that I wouldn't be let down.

2018

Early in January, I received the news that Ann's mom had unexpectedly passed away. She was only 67. I was sad about this, but Spirit had a way to cheer me up. Dana, my realtor, called to tell me that my new place of business would be ready on the 15th of the month! This was fantastic news. I would be able to move in teach a few classes and then leave for Egypt! I thanked Spirit for making everything work out. I felt blessed and relieved.

I sat down to re-evaluate what I needed to buy for the business. Jody's company was moving to another location, so I was able to buy some furniture from her. She also donated a few tables and bookcases, which I was so grateful. I bought chairs for the students and my office. I just needed a few more items. Marikka, my friend from Arizona Images, and I went shopping to get the rest. She was excited to help me decorate and fill the space. We picked up the last of the items that were needed and had a great time while we shopped.

January 15th arrived and so did the movers. Jakki and Christina helped me organize and decorate. Karen, another friend from the spiritual community, helped too. After just a few hours of work, the location was ready. As I closed the door, I looked at the beautiful place and was overjoyed. It was exactly what I wanted. I thanked Spirit, for helping me make this all possible. It truly was a dream come true.

The following night I taught my first class. Marikka and Karen helped me host the classes. I was able to work more closely with the students because I had the extra help. I was so happy that that everything fell into place, and I could breathe again. After teaching a few more classes that first week, I left for Egypt.

I had to change planes a few times, and I finally arrived in Cairo at 1:30 am the next day. I met up with Jakki, and she showed me around our hotel. I told her all I wanted was a shower and some sleep. Not only had I been traveling for 24 hours straight, I was exhausted from all the work that went into moving into my new office!

I took a shower, got in to bed, put on my eye mask and inserted my earplugs. It was close to 3:30 am when I finally fell asleep. I wasn't asleep for long. At 5am, I was awakened by a singing loudly on the intercom! I was so tired that I slurred my words. I asked Jakki who was singing. She told me they were the Egyptian prayers! They were sung throughout the day on an intercom, which just happened to be in the square right outside our balcony! The prayers were so loud that I could hear them with my earplugs in and a pillow over my head. They lasted for almost an hour! I just wanted to sleep! I tried to rest for another hour, but it was useless. I had to get up because we were meeting our group for the tour that day. I was completely sleep deprived and tried to keep myself awake. In my head, I kept telling myself that I could do this, but my body and eyes told a different story!

After getting dressed we met up with the group and had breakfast. Then we saw several sites in Cairo. We visited different temples and saw the skyline of Egypt, including the pyramids, in the distance. I was so elated that I forgot how tired I was! My body kicked into overdrive, and I ran on adrenaline. I stayed awake the entire day and met some wonderful people on the trip. I became fast friends with Nicole, Terrie and Noelle. It turns out that they were very spiritual too! It was a nudge from Spirit.

As the week progressed, we visited many more temples and took an overnight boat down the Nile. We rode camels, saw King Tut's mummy, and experienced the Pyramids at Giza. One morning, at 4 am, we went into the Kings Chamber inside the Great Pyramid. I could feel the energy of all the people that had been there before us. It was incredible to experience, and it is something that I will never forget.

The trip was amazing, and I know I was blessed to be able experience it. There was only one drawback: I came back extremely exhausted and sick. It took me several weeks to recover and settle back into my routine.

In March, I had a grand opening party to celebrate my new location. Nikki came out to help me. Several of my friends helped too. I invited all my clients and students to enjoy the festivities in my new official place of business. In this new space, I was building a spiritual community! I couldn't wait to see what Spirit had in store for me next!

In April, Jakki and I traveled together again. This time it was to Maine to attend John Holland's Advanced Mediumship workshop. I wanted to attend because I wanted to continue developing my Mediumship skills. Plus, I had never been to Maine and wanted to experience its beauty.

Jakki and I flew into Boston and drove to Maine, which would be an hour-and-half drive. We were exhausted by the time we got to the hotel. Sleep could not come fast enough. The workshop started the next morning. It was held at a hotel on the ocean, which was a beautiful backdrop. We met Terry and Anna, two wonderful people, at workshop. We spent a lot time with them. We felt like we had known them before!

As it turned out, they were staying in the room next to ours! We just laughed when we discovered this.

The workshop was a great experience. We made some lasting memories and some great new friends. We said goodbye to our friends but parted knowing would see them soon. They lived in New York, and Jakki and I were going to the ISF conference that was being held there in August. Again, we knew that Spirit played a part in bringing us together.

As the days turned into months, I was busy with CSG. I loved teaching classes to students, and I was grateful that I had my own space to hold classes. The Voice of Spirit had nudged me to get my own place so I could teach more. I thanked Spirit for this because I wouldn't have done it on my own. I also told Spirit that as I learned more, I would continue to teach others. Spirit heard my words and opened more doors for me to learn.

For years, when Nikki and I rented canoes in Las Vegas, we always rented from a man name Les. One day, Les reached out to me about taking some spiritual classes. Les was spiritual and healer. I found this out the last time we rented our canoes from him. His son informed us that his dad would not be taking us to launch our canoes because he was attending his spiritual classes. I was taken aback by this. I told Les' son that I was a Medium. Now it was his turn to be stunned. I told him to have his dad call me because I would be interested in learning more about these spiritual classes. He agreed, and we left it at that.

When I returned to Phoenix I talked to Les about the classes. I told him we would meet up the next time I was in Las Vegas. But we couldn't coordinate our schedules, and we couldn't connect then. Spirit had a hand in helping us connect a few months later.

May was here and Les let me know that he was coming through Phoenix and wanted to meet up. But he wanted me to meet his mentor, Nand, via Skype before his trip. He felt that Nand would be a good mentor for me too. Nand's company, Creative Life Sciences, trains Mediums and healers. He is a clairvoyant, healer, and seer. I told Les to set up the meeting because I was interested. Something just felt right about meeting this man.

Nand, Les, and I connected via Skype a few days later. I immediately connected with Nand, and he felt that he would be a good mentor for me. During this call, Nand taught me some things to help me hone my

Mediumship skills. After the lesson, Nand decided that he was going to come to Phoenix too. I was excited by this opportunity for more training.

A few weeks later, Nand and Les arrived in Phoenix. They both taught me several lessons while they were here. I found out later from Les that Nand had not trained someone with so much knowledge of Mediumship before. Usually his students are beginners. Nevertheless, Nand taught me some different things that I had not learned before. I couldn't wait to add these new tools to the ones I was already using. I loved the classes I had with Nand and Les and continued to take more from time to time.

August was here, and it was finally time for me and Jakki to travel to New York. Terry and Anna picked us up from the airport. We drove to Terry's old neighborhood in New York and had a wonderful Italian dinner. We talked about our Mediumship skills and how we were all growing leaps and bounds. Since the workshop, we met monthly via Zoom to practice our skills together. We all commented on how great it was to see each other in person!

Talk turned to our businesses. We bounced ideas off each other and shared information. We were so involved in our conversation that we had no idea that three hours had passed. It was after 9pm now! We all laughed as we left the restaurant. We went a little Italian grocery store next to the restaurant to get a few treats for our stay. Terry then dropped us off at our Airbnb. Jakki and I were now on our own. Jakki and I explored Manhattan by walking many miles over the next few days. We went to Times Square, Central Park, 911 memorial, and Empire State Building. Jakki hadn't visited the city for many years, so we made sure she saw everything, including the subway! The weather was wonderful, which allowed us to enjoy the city even more.

We had to travel to Stony Brook, New York to attend the ISF conference. I met Coral, who draws Spirit Art, during the first day of the conference. Coral can connect into Loved Ones who are on the Other Side and draw them! I learned this at last year's conference in Scotland. I had wanted a drawing from her, but she didn't have the time. I made sure that I made an appointment with her to get one done this year.

When she met, she kept referring to the person she drew as a "mom." I thought of AP, but it turned out to be a different "mom." Back in my college days, when Ann and I would visit her family in Sedona, I always called her mother "Mom" because that is what she felt like to me. It was "mom" coming through, and I was amazed! I immediately texted Ann to tell her about it. Mom wanted me to know that she was doing well on the Other Side.

The rest of the consisted of learning, healing, and meeting up with old friends. It was fantastic I was able to relax and take some time for myself. I spent as much time in nature as I could, soaking up the beauty of this place. This trip was very much needed because I was really burned out. It gave me the opportunity to recharge because I had been on overdrive since the beginning of the year. Taking this time off helped me connect back in with Spirit.

Once I returned home, I got back into the business groove. I started to teach fall classes and was busy with readings. Jakki and I continued to work with Terry and Anna on practicing our skills each month. I also continued to take more classes. Time flew by and months passed.

In December, Sandy and his friend Eleanor taught a weekend workshop at my business. It was called The Foundations of Spiritual Studies. My students were excited to meet both teachers because Gordon Smith had been their teachers. I always recommend his book to my Intuitive Studies students. Plus, most of the students had never had a teacher from Scotland. I always tell my students to get a variety of instructors because everyone can teach you something new! The weekend workshop was amazing. The students loved it so much that we planned part two for the next year.

After the workshop, we had a few days off and took full advantage of it. We visited diners because Sandy loves to eat that type of food! I took them to Sedona to see the beautiful red mountains. And we rode the Polar Express in Williams, Arizona. The Polar Express is an adaption of the movie, and it helps to get you in the holiday spirit. It was the first time for all of us, and we thoroughly enjoyed it. After experiencing the Polar Express, we all felt ready for Christmas to come.

Sandy and Eleanor were returning to Scotland the next day. We said our goodbyes knowing we would see each other the following year. I thanked Spirit for having them come because our discussions gave me a new outlook on my Mediumship. I had been suffering from burnout and was having a hard time with my work. Visiting with them helped me to recharge and see things from a different perspective which Spirit knew I needed.

A few weeks later Spirit brought another friend to help me with this too. Terry was traveling to Sedona with her husband for the holidays. Even though we both were not feeling well, we met up for tea and French fries. We laughed at the combo, but the salt from the fries helped our sore throats! Terry offered me some good advice about work that helped me think differently too. We also talked about how Spirit had brought us together this year and how very grateful we both were. Spirit knew we would have a kinship and would be lifelong friends.

2019

January rolled in, and I was busy taking more online Mediumship classes. There was a total of 30 classes that I was taking to earn another certificate. I dug in and tried to do a class a day, including homework. My schedule was tight, but I wanted to finish as many as I could before I started teaching my spring semester classes.

It was a grueling schedule, but I completed all the classes and received my certificate in six weeks. I was proud of the fact that I was able to get it completed so quickly, but my energy was drained. It took me a few weeks before I felt back to normal. I knew that I needed to take it easy and give myself a break. So, for the next few months I just focused on giving readings and teaching classes.

In March, a friend posting on Facebook about a Spirit Artist who drew pictures of Spirit Guides. I an "urge" to have a drawing. I sent a message via Facebook to Ellen, the artist. I asked her if she would draw my Spirit Guides who helped me with my work as a Medium. I told her that I knew that I had more than one, but I felt that I needed to see who they were. Ellen responded to me immediately and was up to the task. She was excited to draw whoever came through for me. In turn, I was excited to see what they looked like. I didn't know it then, but it was a nudge from Spirit.

Two weeks later, I had a Skype reading with Ellen. She showed me the drawing of my three guides. Then she shared some information about them. The first one was a Native American who had been a healer. The second one was an Oracle from Greece. The third one was my great grandmother Beatrice. I knew that I had a Native American guide, but the other two astonished me. I was told by Joy, from the YAYA group that I had had a past life in Greece. I had been an Oracle there. Let's not forget that I am Greek too!

I didn't really know my grandmother, so I didn't even know her mother's name. But I always had an affinity for the name "Beatrice" and had no idea why. Now it made sense! After the Skype call, I verified my great grandmother's name through Ancestry. It was Beatrice! I texted Ellen and gave her the validation!

Since I now knew her name, I felt that I needed to talk to her. I told her that I was grateful that she was working with me. I also told her that I couldn't wait to find out more information about her. Another nudge from Spirit.

I went to see Nikki in April. We canoed down the Colorado River with her neighbors for a few days. Being in nature always helps me to recharge, and I felt rejuvenated. I was so happy to get away for a few days because I had been feeling burnt out again. I took this time to relax and enjoy life.

I received my Spirit Guide drawing in the mail when I returned home. Once I saw it, I had an "urge" to start writing my book. It was like my guides were telling me to write! I didn't know what I was going to write about, so I pushed it off.

A week later, Spirit told me to "write," but this time it was louder. Then my out of the blue, several students told me to write. After that, I picked an Oracle card and that card said "write." I finally had enough! I told Spirit that I would write but needed some time. I felt that I needed some assistance.

I called Jakki and told her I was going to write, but I didn't know what I would write about. I told her that I wanted to write about my different experiences, and she informed me that I was writing a memoir. I had never thought about writing about my life, but this now made sense! A few days later, I started to write. I committed to completing a page a day. I didn't realize how easily it was to write a page a day! The words just started to flow. It was magical.

I couldn't believe how much I had written in just a few weeks! And I couldn't believe how writing healed past wounds. I realized that this book was going to help me in more ways than one, and it was a blessing. However, I had a recurring thought I felt was odd. I just knew in my heart that this book would not be published until my mother passed. I didn't know why I felt this way, but I did. It was the Voice of Spirit.

I was going to see Nikki again at the end of May. I was going to fly into to Las Vegas, and we were going to drive to California together. I thought of my mother a few days before the trip. I asked myself, "Do I have any unresolved issues with her?" It was a strange thought, but I let it go. I knew in my heart that I had closure with my mother, and I didn't have any unresolved issues. I went on with my day. I didn't know it at the time, but it was the Voice of Spirit again.

Nikki and I a great time in California. It was a soul recharge that I needed. I drove back with Nikki and flew out late one night. I read for clients the next day and taught a class. Life was good, but that changed dramatically the next day.

I woke up and did my usual routine. I only had thing on my schedule: a dentist appointment. In the middle of my cleaning, I receive a call from Nikki. I couldn't answer because the hygienist was scraping my teeth. Then Nikki sent me a text saying it was an emergency. This was not something that Nikki did. I knew something was very wrong! I stopped my cleaning and called her right back.

She was hysterical and told me that she had someone check on mom at her apartment. When they found her, she wasn't breathing! I asked, "Is she dead?" Through her tears, she said that she didn't know, but the paramedics were on their way. I told her that I would go check on the situation when my cleaning was finished.

When it was done, I called Nikki. She was still crying when she answered and told me that our mom had died of a heart attack in her sleep. I immediately knew that she was in a better place and could finally start to live. Nikki and I talked for a while She told me that she couldn't believe that Mom was gone. She just had had a visit with her two weeks before. For me it was a bit surreal. I remembered my thoughts of her the previous when and while I was the writing this book. I realized it was the Voice of Spirit trying to prepare me for her death. Since the news of my mother came so late in the day, I couldn't cancel my class that night. I knew that Spirit meant for it to be that way.

I informed the students in my monthly development circle about my mother's passing. They were so kind. They asked if I was okay having class that night. I told them that I was and that there was a reason the class was tonight. When we opened the circle, my mother came to seven of the eight students as well as to me. She apologized for the things that had happened in our lives. My mother said that now that she was free from the shackles that bound her in this world, she would have lived life differently. As I listened to this evidence, I knew that she had gone through her "life review" on the Other Side.

During a life review, a soul who passes reviews their life with their guides and teachers to see how they performed here on Earth. It is like watching a movie of your life. You see your actions and how they affected others here on Earth. My mother went through hers and saw how it affected me. She saw that I had forgiven her years ago and now understood why I had to step away from her. This made me happy because she now knew how I felt. I always wished her the best even though I walked away. I was grateful that she came to me so quickly to let me know that she was on the Other Side. She was finally free! Not only did she come through, but Jerry and Steve came too! I was grateful for all the messages that night. Spirit had purposefully had me hold that class for the messages to come through. What a blessing it was!

I called Nikki to share the messages that came through from our mother. She was amazed and happy that she had made it to the Other Side. Then Nikki told me that she would be in Phoenix in three days. She needed help to go through our mother's stuff and to find her will. I told her that I would help her in any way that she needed.

Nikki arrived that weekend. We wanted to get a jump start on things and went to my mother's an hour after her arrival. Leslie from Rising Phoenix and her husband Cal came to help us. My mother's house was packed; there were things everywhere. It took some time, but we found the will and other paperwork that Nikki needed. Nikki was having a hard time processing everything. She couldn't do too much, so I just went into a cleaning mode to get things organized. Going through her things was surreal. My mother still had items that I remembered from my childhood.

We were there for a few hours that first day and returned the following day. There was a lot of things to go through. All the hard work paid off because we found a few treasures. One of the treasures was a book that my grandmother made. She was 13 when she had made the book. It was about her life and showed pictures of her mom and dad (my great grandparents), Beatrice and Charles. I couldn't believe it, because I had just received the Spirit guide drawing of Beatrice! Nikki and I compared the drawing to the photos. They showed the same person. We were blown away.

The book revealed that Beatrice had been born in Montreal. I have always had an "urge" to see that city! I also learned that her husband Charles who was born in Illinois but his father Isaac, which is my great-great grandfather, was born in Edinburgh, Scotland. I had visited Edinburgh before and had such an affinity for this city. Now I knew why! I even had plans to visit this city again a few months after my mother's passing. Nikki and I were grateful that we finally see pictures of our great grandparents and were amazed by the synchronicity of it all. It was the Voice of Spirit connecting all the pieces together.

When we finished going through everything, Nikki decided to bury our mom. She had read her will and acted according to our mother's wishes. Nikki organized a quick viewing and had her body shipped back to Wisconsin, where her plot was located. I didn't attend the view or the burial because I didn't want to remember my mother that way. In my heart I knew that I had had closure with her. I had already let go.

Nikki returned home two weeks after the funeral. She told me about the people who had attended the funeral to give their respects. She connected with her godmother who she hadn't seen or spoken to since she was a little girl. This made me think of Donna, my godmother. When we moved to Arizona my mother lost contact with most of her friends, including Donna. I hadn't spoken to her since I was about 13 years old. I tried to remember her last name, but it seemed to elude me. I asked my mother and Spirit to help me remember.

A few days later as I lay in bed, I remembered Donna's last name! I looked her up on the internet and contacted her. We had a great time, quickly catching up. It was difficult for her to speak. She was scheduled for vocal cord surgery in a few days. I told her to rest her voice and promised that we speak more after the surgery.

A week later, Donna's son Cody sent me a Facebook friend request. He was with his mother to take her in for surgery. One night while they were going through old photos and found one of me. She told him that she had just spoken to me. He couldn't believe it. He immediately looked for me on Facebook. I was so excited to connect in with him again. Cody was like a brother to me... we share the same birthday. I accepted the friend request, and we spoke a few days later. We caught up on our lives and made plans to visit each other soon. I was so happy that I was able to reconnect with them. I know that my mother played a part in this, which made me smile. She was already helping me from the Other Side.

The following week I kept getting the "urge" to contact my friend Terry. I had been so drained; I hadn't reached out to tell her about my mom. I sent her a text asking about when we could get together to practice our Mediumship skills. She sent me back a note and wanted to know how Jakki and I were. I gave her the news about my mother. She immediately called me.

I found out that she and her father had the same type of relationship. Terry could relate to how I was feeling. She even shared a story that she spoke about at his funeral. It could have been my story. It was identical to how I felt about my mother. I was so grateful that someone knew how I felt. Even though we didn't have the best relationship, I still loved her. It felt like I was going through a divorce. Terry completely understood. As we spoke, we both knew that my mother was instrumental in having Terry contact me. She was helping me again, and I felt blessed.

At the time of this writing, it has been a month since my mother passed. I've been going through a whirlwind of emotions, but I have been able to reflect on her life. I have thanked Spirit for helping me work through my journey of life with her. I realize now that I learned a lot walking this path with her. My mother was my greatest teacher.

We all have lessons to learn while we are here on Earth. My mother's role was to show me the things I should not do! This has put me on the path I am traveling today. I would not be where I am without those lessons. As I write this, tears are streaming down my face because I have love in my heart for her.

I know now that my relationship with her will be better. It took her passing to release what pain was left inside, and for that I am truly grateful. I have thanked her for her part in my journey and sent her love and blessings. She can now be free from the chains that bound her in this lifetime. As for me, I can now speak my truth with her because she can finally listen and can now assist me in my work as a Medium from the Other Side. It is the best of both worlds, and the relationship that I always wanted. I am grateful for the journey that lies ahead for us. We will now be on the same page and going in the same direction!

As for me, my story will continue. I will continue to take classes and expand my knowledge and Mediumship skill sets. I will pass this information on to my students for them to grow too. I will continue to expand CSG with readings, healings, and classes. I will also work on balancing my work and personal life. I still remember the prediction from the man from New Orleans, and he hasn't been wrong yet! I am going to focus on bringing in the third man for a romantic relationship. I know that more adventures lie ahead, and I am grateful for all that awaits. Thank you for allowing me to share my story of how I was *Guided by the Voice of Spirit*!

APPENDIX

EVIDENTIAL MEDIUMSHIP

Over the five years that I have been working with Spirit, I have received some great evidential evidence as a Medium. When I give readings, sometimes I just shake my head because Spirit <u>always</u> amazes me. The evidence that is brought forward can literally be anything! This could be that their Loved Ones are alive on the Other Side, acknowledging something of the past or present, apologies, advice, their favorite memories, and everything in between. Everyone is different and no communicator is the same.

It is my job as a Medium to interpret the messages given and pass them on to the clients. I am just the vessel in the process, a conduit for the Loved One who has passed. I find that this work helps to heal the hearts of many of my clients, and I love being a part of that healing. Not to mention letting them know that their Loved Ones are alive on the Other Side. I want to share some examples of evidence that I have received while giving messages to my clients over the years. I have read for thousands of people and am still in awe of the presence of Spirit.

I do want to note that I don't remember most things that I have said in my readings because I am merely the vessel. I tell clients that after their reading it is like I am erased. I might remember just bits and pieces of the reading if I remember anything at all! The reason for this is that I would have libraries of people's evidence. That information is not for me, it is for the client. The noted evidence below are reminders to me by clients after a reading, reviews, or evidence that Spirit has helped me to recall.

<u>Acknowledgement That Are Loved Ones Are Still Alive</u>
<u>Jackie</u>

Jackie has been a client for several years. Once when she was booking an appointment, it was six weeks before I could see her. I am typically booked up and clients may have to schedule reading weeks in advance. When Jackie's appointment arrived, she was the first client I was seeing that day. Another woman was with her, and I noticed that they both were very sad.

I thought this was a bit odd because Jackie normally comes by herself, and she is usually a very happy person. Jackie asked me if Michelle could listen in on the reading. I agreed, and we sat down for her reading. I wasn't sure who Michelle was or why they were both so sad, but I found out as soon I started Jackie's reading. Sarah, who was married to Jackie, came through. She told me that she had committed suicide the day before. Sarah wanted to apologize to Jackie about what had happened and to say that she loved her. She wanted "both" of them to know that she was fine, alive, and free.

Jackie and Michelle were relieved and grateful that Sarah had made it to the Other Side. Michelle, who turned out to be Sarah's sister, was a very religious person. She said that she wasn't sure if Sarah would "go to heaven" because she had committed suicide. Sarah wanted Michelle to know that she was in heaven and that it didn't matter how she got there! As I told them this, I could see and feel the healing that was taking place for both. Their demeanors changed, and they began to cheer up. I commented on how timely the reading had been. Jackie may have scheduled the reading weeks before, but it was <u>exactly</u> the day that she needed a message. Spirit helped Jackie and Michelle to receive closure from Sarah's passing.

Danielle

Danielle, another client, came to see me because she wanted to connect with her nephew, who had passed tragically. Initially, she was skeptical but felt she needed to try it out. As I read for Danielle, a male came through. He told me that he had passed away from a motorcycle accident. He shared me some very detailed facts about the accident. Then he told me that Danielle was questioning if it was an "accident" at all. He said the accident could have been prevented and that there was some cover up that took place after his death. Of course, I didn't know any of this information prior to the reading. Danielle immediately started to cry when I was shared this evidence. After the reading, Danielle told me that I had validated what she had been questioning the entire time. She was overjoyed that her nephew was still alive and with her. She told me that she could finally feel a bit of peace knowing that he was doing okay.

Rachel

Sometimes, Spirit sends clients to me. People have told me that they feel an "urge" to get a reading and ultimately find me on the internet. This was the case for Rachel. Rachel's friend had recently had a reading with me that gave her closure. Rachel wasn't sure how she felt about readings but decided to give it a try. She went to my website and read about me. She wanted to see if she could find closure too.

Rachel and I did a reading over the phone. Her son and his girlfriend came through to me. Her son had been driving when the car swerved and went off the road. They were both killed instantly. He said that there was alcohol and drugs involved and that his girlfriend had been pregnant. Rachel could not believe the evidence I was sharing with her. Again, I didn't know any of this information before I read for her. I heard her crying and blowing her nose. She confirmed that there had been a tragic accident related to drugs and alcohol and that the car had swerved off the road.

I continued to receive more evidence from her son. He told me that she was wearing his shoes. She just laughed and admitted that she had been wearing his slippers since he passed. He then said that his mom was not living life. He said she was always going into his room and nothing was moved. He wanted her to start to live! And he wanted her to clean out his room. He called it a "mausoleum." Rachel validated all this evidence. She said she would honor his request and would start to go through his things.

When the reading was finished, Rachel was so happy that they were alive. She told me that she had not been a believer before the reading but was now. She was in awe because there was no way I knew anything about her or her son. Plus, I was reading with her over the phone and could not see her. She continues to receive readings with me and referred the mother of her son's girlfriend to read with me too.

Loved Ones Who Came to Give Messages to the Other Person in the Room
Susan and Anthony

Sometimes a client will make an appointment for themselves, but the reading turns out to be for the person who came with them. This was the case with Susan. A client had referred Susan to me because she needed closure for her stepson. Susan came with her husband, Anthony. He was very skeptical but was there for support. The only thing that I knew prior to the reading was that a referral was coming to me. I didn't know the person's name. Susan had booked a reading through the website and asked if her husband would be able to listen. I agreed and saw them a few weeks later.

As the reading started, a son came through. I realized that the reading was for Anthony, not Susan. The son called his father "Pops." Anthony almost fell off his chair. He was astonished because that was the *only name* that his son ever called him. Anthony began crying hysterically. I asked him if he wanted to continue, and he said please do.

His son told me about a tragic accident that took place. He said someone had hurt him. He said that at the time he was murdered, he had made the phone ring. His father had answered, but there was no one on the other end. Anthony was in shock and couldn't believe that I knew about the phone. I brought in more evidence from his son.

He said they were supposed to celebrate his and his stepmother's birthday, but the celebrations never happened because of his passing. He said he wanted them to go out to celebrate the birthdays. The son also knew about all the people that were honoring him because was a firefighter. Anthony was stunned. He validated the birthdays and that his was son being honored.

After the reading, Anthony continued crying and gave me the biggest hug. He told me that this reading gave him the closure that he needed. Anthony knew without a doubt that his son was alive on the Other Side. Anthony also said that he was no longer a skeptic because no one knew the evidence that I provided.

Brenda and Ken

Spirit brought me another client, Brenda. When Brenda booked her reading, it was for weeks later. When I met with Brenda, she asked if her husband Ken could listen. I agreed. I started to read for Brenda, but nothing I said to her made sense. Occasionally clients do not understand the evidence that I provide. If this happens, I will tell the client that I will give them a few more pieces of evidence. If they still do not understand, then I will stop the reading. I do this is because the connection in the link might not be good, the client is not open, or I am not the right Medium for them. Not to mention I don't want to waste their time or mine.

I gave her a few more pieces of evidence, but she still couldn't understand it. So, I ended the reading. I got up and apologized to Brenda because I couldn't connect in with her energy. As I said this, I heard, "Tell them I am here, it's your dad." I shared the message and Ken began to cry. Brenda told me that his Ken's father had passed away and that he missed him. I asked Ken if he wanted a reading with his father. He said, "Yes!"

I connected with Ken's father, and I gave him some evidence, which included his watch and being a cop. Tears rolled down Kens' face. Ken had tears rolling down his eyes. Hearing the evidence stunned him. He validated that he had his father's watch, which he treasured. He also told me that he was a cop. Ken said that his father had passed decades before Ken had gone to the police academy.

After the reading, Ken told me that he had been skeptical at first, but now knew for a fact that this was real. He even apologized for being skeptical! I told him that it was okay, I am just the vessel. It is not my job to make you believe, it's just my job to just give you the messages. He laughed. Ken told me that hearing that his father was proud of him was the best thing he could ever have heard.

Giving Loved Ones Signs
Lisa

Loved Ones who have passed give us signs to show us that they are with us. This was evident when Lisa came to see me for a reading.

Lisa's husband came through. He said that he had passed after a years-long battle with cancer. He also gave evidence about to a birthday cake and cuckoo clock. I had no idea what he meant but I shared what I received with Lisa. She began crying, and her mouth dropped.

She validated that her husband had had a rare type of cancer that took over his life for several years. But what she told me next shocked me. Lisa said he had passed on the night of her was her birthday. She knew that he would want her to eat the cake that he had bought her, so she cut a slice for herself and her mom. At that very moment, the cuckoo clock started to "cuckoo." Lisa said that the clock hadn't worked in years. She felt that it was him that night. Lisa was overjoyed that I was able to validate that it was him that night.

Melissa

Spirit has a way of making things happen when we need to hear from our Loved Ones. This was the case for Melissa. Her daughter had emailed, wanting to book a reading for her mom. I told her that I was booked out several weeks and gave her the earliest appointment that I had. She replied, saying that the day that I had available was the day she was supposed to give birth. She was hoping to get an appointment for her mom sooner. I told her that I would let her know if something came up in the next few weeks.

After responding, I asked Spirit to please open an appointment for Melissa if she needed to see me sooner. A week later a cancellation came up, and I was able to get her in. I always tell clients that Spirit will get people in if they really need to see me. I met Melissa and her daughter. As I read for Melissa, I could tell that she wasn't open to receiving the reading, so I asked the angels to help Melissa open-up to hear the message. As soon as I, asked her stepdad and biological dad came through to give her evidence. Finally, her mom came through. That was the person that Melissa wanted to hear from.

Her mother said that she had had cancer that took over her body. She said that Melissa had been her caregiver, and she wanted to say, "Thank you." She said that she was giving Melissa a bird as a sign that she was there. Melissa looked at me dumbfounded when I shared this evidence. She validated that her mother had had cancer and that she took care of her for a few years.

Then laughed. She told me that she had recently been seeing hummingbird at her window each day. She said she started to see the bird every day when she moved her office into her mom's room! Her mom gave me more evidence to validate that she was with her, including a comment about Tupperware. Once I relayed that to Melissa, she burst out laughing. She told me that she had recently tried to go through her mom's

Tupperware, but it was overwhelming. She gave up and shoved it all back in the cabinet. Her mom wanted to let her know that she was with her and that she should not to give up on that or life.

She told me that Melissa was depressed and was not moving forward. I relayed the evidence to Melissa. She couldn't believe it. She told me that this was exactly what was happening in her life. Melissa's entire demeanor changed after the reading. She gave me a hug and thanked me profusely. She told me that she was going to start to live life now. Melissa said that her daughter's new baby was coming soon, and she had to be the grandma! She said that she would honor her mom and start to live again!

Jennifer

Jennifer needed closure from a passed Loved One, so Spirit sent her to me.

Jennifer was referred to me by another client of mine. As I started Jennifer's reading, her grandmother came through and gave me some wonderful evidence. However, I felt that something was off.

Jennifer's grandmother said that Jennifer wanted to connect with someone else, and then a male stepped in. This turned out to be Jennifer's son, who had passed way because of an overdose. He wanted his mom to know that he was doing fine. He said that he was sorry that he hadn't listened to his mother, who had warned him something bad was going to happen if he didn't change his ways. Tears rolled down her face as I shared the evidence. As I started Jennifer's reading, I had her grandmother who came through. She gave me some wonderful evidence, but I knew that something was off. She validated that it was true.

Jennifer's son also said that he came to her in lyrics, and she started to smile. He made me think of Ed Sheeran playing his guitar. I told Jennifer about this, and she started to laugh. Ed Sheeran was one of the songs that reminded her of her son. After the reading, Jennifer said that she felt at peace and was thankful he came through. She was happy that he was with her grandmother and that he was coming to visit her too.

Loved Ones' Knowledge of an Object that the Client Brought
Laura

Many times, when clients come for reading, they will bring an item that belonged to the Loved One that passed. This was the case with Laura.

Laura was a sweet woman with an accent. Laura had just moved to Phoenix for Michigan. Her a grandmother came through during her reading. The grandmother told me that Laura was looking for love and wanted a tall, dark handsome man. I told Laura this, and she cried and laughed at the same time! This was her favorite grandmother and she was happy that she was connecting in with her. Plus, she confirmed that she was looking for a tall dark handsome man to date!

Her grandmother gave me more evidence, but it was the item that Laura brought with her that was the clincher. I didn't know this, but Laura had her grandmother's necklace in her bag. Her grandmother told me that the beautiful necklace belonged to her and that Laura has it now. When I told Laura this, she cried and pulled the necklace out of her bag. She told me that if I spoke of a necklace, then she knew that this reading was real.

Laura told me after the reading that she was always skeptical but had felt a need to get a reading. Her grandmother had been urging her to get it done. Laura was thrilled with the reading and thanked me for connecting with her grandmother. I have seen Laura several times since then, and her grandmother continues to give her advice for her journey ahead.

Jamie

Spirit also brought Jaime to me. Jamie's friend is a client, and Jaime came to write down all the notes from her friend's reading. I loved Jamie's energy when I met her. She was a gentle woman who was open to receiving a message.

As I started the reading, I brought through Jamie's mother, who she desperately wanted to hear from. Her mother told me that Jaime was very close to her and wanted to check to see how she was doing. Jamie's mom said that she had lost a fight with cancer and that her last years of life were hard. She went on to say she was fine, but also talking about a photo and a horse. I relayed this evidence to Jamie, who started to laugh.

Jamie opened her bag and pulled out a photo of her mother and a horse. She showed me the horse's bridle, which she had brought too. Jamie told me that she loved her horse, but it had passed years before. The message from her mom was that she and her horse were doing just fine. Jamie validated that all she wanted to know is that they were okay. Jamie was so happy to hear from her mom and to know that she was with her beloved horse.

Tracey

Tracey is another client Spirit sent to me. Tracey's daughter wanted a reading and talked her mom into getting one too. They had just moved to Phoenix and found me via the internet. The daughter called and asked for two appointments for later that day. I told her that I was unfortunately booked out several weeks but would let them know if a cancellation came up.

I knew booking two back-to-back appointments would be tough. But Spirit wanted me to read for them, then something would open. Later that week, a client canceled her and a friend's appointment due to sickness. I knew Spirit had a hand in this, and I slotted Tracey and her daughter in for the appointments.

I read for Tracey first. I could tell from her demeanor that she was very closed off to hearing a message. When someone is closed off, I ask the angels to help open the person up. It took a bit, but it worked. I had brought through her grandfather and gave her evidence, but I could tell there was someone else that she wanted to hear from. At that moment, her son came through.

This boy was not her biological son, but he called her "mom." He told me that he was in a car accident and had tragically passed away. The son kept telling me about his hair. I had no idea what that meant. When I shared this evidence with Tracey, her eyes widened, and her demeanor changed. She started to cry and validated the evidence. Then she reached in her pocket and showed me a piece of his hair that she had brought with her. She just looked at me with amazement. The angels helped me give her the message that she was so desperately wanting to hear.

After the reading Tracey told me that she was very skeptical of Mediums and had waited six years before getting this reading. Before the reading, she told herself that if this was real, then her son would mention his hair. Tracey gave me a big hug and told me that I changed her life. She knew without a doubt that her son was alive and that he was with her.

Loved Ones' Knowledge of Gifts or Giving Gifts
Amy

During readings, Loved Ones will share knowledge of gifts that were given to them after they have passed. This was the case with a client named Amy.

Amy had wanted to schedule three readings for her and family members. Her husband had recently passed, and she wanted to connect in with him. I always tell clients that there is "no guarantee" that I can bring a certain Loved One through, but I always ask my guide Teddy. If he gives me the okay, then I book the reading. Teddy told me that I would be able to connect into the husband, so we scheduled the three readings.

A few weeks later, I met with Amy, her daughter, and sister-in-law for their readings. When several people coming together, I still read each person separately, but I allow everyone to listen to each other's readings. When I started the first reading with Amy, her husband immediately stepped in. He told me that he had battled with the cancer for some time and that his body just gave out. He was alive and happy on the Other Side, cancer free. I relayed this evidence to Amy and she just cried. I gave her more evidence from her husband and then switched to read for the daughter. They both cried but felt a sense of peace because they knew that he was fine.

When I read for his sister however, they were overjoyed. He shared that they had honored him with a beautiful grave site. He then talked about a wind chime. I didn't know what this meant but relayed the evidence to his sister. They all gasped. The sister said that she had just placed a beautiful wind chime at his grave. After the readings, the sister showed me the photo of the grave with the wind chime she had recently added. They were all happy that he was well and knew that he was watching over all of them.

Paula

Soon after, I read for a woman named Paula. Since it was a phone reading, I had no idea what she looked like or how old she was. When I began reading for her, I felt that she was in her early 20s. A father stepped in and wanted to give her a message. He said that she and a few others were very distraught over his passing. The father also shared that she and a few others recently visited his grave. I relayed this evidence to Paula, and she validated that this was correct.

However, I could tell in her voice that she was still skeptical. Then she asked me what she found at the grave. When this happens, I am very honest with clients. I tell them that I am here to give evidence, not play a guessing game. I let them know that if the Loved One shares the evidence with me, then I relay it to you. If a Medium start searching for the evidence, the link with Spirit is dropped and then you are working psychically. Paula sighed when I told her this. But her father did not disappoint her.

He said that they had found three coins by his headstone. The coins were gifts from him, one for each person. When I told Paula, she immediately started crying. She told me that she, her sister, and her cousin recently went to visit his grave and found three coins. She was overjoyed because she now knew that her father was with her.

After the reading, Paula told me that she was trying to "test" me to see if I was the "real deal." I told Paula that I was happy to give her the message from her father, but readings work best if you are open and not trying to test the Medium. When that happens, you put a block up in your reading, and it's hard for the Medium to deliver the message to you quickly and easily. And sometimes you may not get the evidence that you are looking for from the Loved One because the Loved One might want to communicate other things. Or the evidence you want may not be in the Medium's dictionary. She apologized and said she would be open for her next reading. She also told me that she was grateful for the reading and that I was able to give her closure for her father's passing.

Loved Ones Giving Advice or Warnings
Mary

When I am working with clients' Loved Ones, I receive all types of evidence. Many times, I am unaware of why the evidence is given. I never question this evidence; I just relay it. If a client does not know what the evidence means, I advise them to write it down because it will be revealed later. This was the case for a client named Mary.

This was the second reading I did for Mary. It was done over the phone. Throughout the reading, I provided her with evidence, but the end part of the reading was most poignant. Mary's grandmother told me to tell her about macaroni and cheese and broken bones. I tried to clarify what this would mean to Mary, but she wouldn't tell me anything more. I shared this evidence with Mary, and she got annoyed. She told me that she didn't understand why I would tell her these things and became very upset.

I asked my guide, Teddy, what I should do. He told me to offer this reading free of charge and advise her to write this information down. I did exactly what Teddy told me and left it at that. I was feeling perplexed when we ended the call. I didn't understand the evidence or why Mary became upset. I decided that I had to just let it go.

Fast forward to a year later. One night as I was going to bed, Mary popped up in my head. I had not thought of her since that reading. I didn't know why I was thinking of her at that point, but Spirit knew. I received an email from Mary the next day. She wanted to apologize to me. She wrote that when she received her reading, she thought I was a "crazy psychic." However, now she wanted me to know that the information I gave to her came to pass. Her father fell down the stairs and broke several bones. As he was recuperating, he only wanted to eat macaroni and cheese!

Mary offered to pay for that reading, plus she wanted to schedule another one. I read this and was stunned. I realized that the message from her grandmother had been a warning. I was happy that Mary reached out to me to validate the evidence. I have read for Mary, and several people she has referred to me, over the years.

Joe

Joe also received a warning from his Loved One. Joe's sister referred him to me. He put off reading with me for some time, but finally relented. He told his sister to make an appointment. A few weeks, later I read for Joe over the phone.

I immediately brought through his grandmother. Joe was completely overwhelmed because that was the person he wanted to connect with. His grandmother said that she had taken care of him as a young boy and was worried about him. She said that he was having problems with his jaw and teeth. I shared this evidence with Joe, and he validated it. Joe told me that he didn't have the money to see the doctor. His grandmother then said that he needed to book an appointment immediately. He could figure out the money situation afterward. She continued, saying that he would be alright, but that this had to be done. The grandmother made him promise that he would take care of it right away.

She also told me that she had been "pushing" him to have a reading with me. I shared this with Joe, and he laughed laugh. He said he had been feeling an "urge" to have a reading with me. He was so happy to hear from his grandmother during the reading and thanked me profusely. And he told me that he was going to make an appointment with a doctor the next day.

Joe's sister came to see me a few weeks later. She said that Joe wanted to thank me because the doctor found stage 1 cancer in his jaw. The doctor said that it was a good thing that it was caught before it started to spread. I was taken aback by this, but I realized Joe's grandmother had given him a warning. I was happy that she urged him to get an appointment. I also was grateful that I happened to be the vessel to share the message with Joe.

Lori

Spirit inspired another client, Lori, to book a reading. Lori had had a dream of her grandfather and felt that he had a message for her. The next day, she went on the internet to find a Medium. She was led to my website and booked a phone reading with me. Of course, I didn't know any of this information until after the reading was completed.

Both of Lori's grandfathers stepped in when the reading began. One grandfather told me that Lori was looking at his picture, and the other grandfather told me that he had come to her in a dream. She validated the evidence and was stunned. Then the grandfather who had visited in the dream shared that her daughter was having stomach issues. He said that Lori was giving her milk of magnesia. He wanted her to stop this. He said that it was not good for the girl's stomach because of an allergy. He suggested that Lori investigate giving her herbs instead. I relayed all this evidence to Lori, and she was amazed. She confirmed that she was giving her daughter this exact medicine and that she was allergic to many things. Lori was grateful that her grandfather came to give her the message to help treat her daughter's stomach issues.

Lauren

Lauren was a client for year. When her father passed, she came with her daughter and niece for a reading. Her father immediate came through at that reading. He shared how he passed, which Lauren confirmed. Then he told me about Lauren's house and flies. I had no idea what he was trying to tell me, but I told her what I received. Lauren looked at me blankly while her daughter and niece busted out laughing.

Lauren's daughter said that she had been telling her mom to move because flies were infesting her house. Her father went on to share that there was a problem with a pipe, so she needed to put the house on the market soon. Lauren just shook her head. She had been trying to decide if she should move or not. She knew that her father knew a lot about pipes and houses and that he was giving her a warning.

Lauren thanked me and said she would update on what happened with the house. I heard from Lauren a few months later. She said that she had sold her house. Right after the sale went through, a sewer pipe burst right outside of her backyard. Lauren was so thankful that her dad had warned her. She said she would have had a big mess to deal with if she hadn't put the house on the market as her father suggested.

Loved Ones Acknowledging Things After They Have Passed
Joanne

Our Loved Ones are still aware of things after they have passed to the Other Side. When giving readings, I often receive acknowledgments of these things from the Loved Ones. This was the case for a woman named Joanne.

Joanne had been scheduling phone readings for years. She loved hearing from her mom in her readings. Even though her mom had passed away some time ago, she was still sorting through her things. During one reading, Joanne's mom came through to acknowledge things that she was doing. Her mom told me about her glasses that Joanne was using. I relayed this to Joanne, and she laughed. She told me that she recently had found her mother's designer glasses in some boxes. She changed out the prescription lens in them so she could wear them.

Then her mother acknowledged the lemon trees. When I shared this evidence with Joanne, she laughed again. She said that she had recently moved on to her mom's property and that there were wonderful lemon trees there. She said that her mom must be acknowledging them because they were starting to ripen. Joanne left the reading happy that her mother had acknowledged these things. Joanne was sure her mother was still with her.

Tammy

Tammy, a client, came to see me for a reading. She said she was looking for advice. I was focused on her question, but a Loved One wanted to step in. I shared this with Tammy, and she said she would be open to receiving a message. So, I brought in this male who turned out to be her father-in-law.

Tammy's father-in-law spoke about the London Bridge and then played the London Bridge song in my mind. I wasn't sure why he was talking about this, but I shared this evidence with her. Tammy couldn't believe it. She laughed. She said that her husband had a job interview in Lake Havasu, Arizona, which is where the original London Bridge is now located. Her husband's father wanted to acknowledge that his son was going for this interview and was wishing him luck.

Danielle

Spirit made sure that Danielle had a reading with me. Danielle had booked an appointment with me weeks in advance, but her appointment landed on the same day as her niece's birthday party. Danielle rescheduled, but the new date didn't work out either. I told her that I would put her name on my cancellation list. She informed me that because of her work schedule, she could only see me for the last appointment of the day. As I wrote her name the cancellation list, I asked Spirit to make things work out if she really needed to read with me.

That is exactly what happened a week later. One day, the last appointment opened, and Danielle was able come in. Danielle's brother stepped in and told me that he was the one pushing her to have this reading. He shared that she had been having a hard time since his passing, and she just needed to see joy again. I relayed this evidence to Danielle, and tears rolled down her face. She said that she loved her brother and missed him so much. Danielle also validated that she had been feeling an "urge" to read with me and now understood why.

I continued to share evidence with Danielle, but it was one piece that completely stunned her. Her brother shared that he had been driving with her and that certain songs would come on the radio reminded her of him. I relayed this evidence to Danielle, and she validated it. However, it was a few minutes later when Danielle really *understood* the message and started to laugh hysterically. She said that his ashes had been in the back of her car for over a year now. Danielle said that he was "literally" driving around with her! We both laughed. As tears continued to roll down her face, she said that this was exactly what she needed. Her brother was a funny man, and she missed him terribly. Danielle told me that he always made her laugh and that was exactly what happened in her reading.

Dates or Names Being Given by the Loved One
Tracey

When giving readings, I receive many numbers from Loved Ones. These numbers refer to birthdays, dates when someone passed, ages, favorite numbers, number of children, etc. Names, however, are rarer for me.

Sometimes a Loved One will share a name or just an initial. This was the case with Tracey.

Earlier, I wrote about how Tracey's son came through and told her about his hair. The son was not the only person who came through that day. One of her ex-boyfriends wanted to give a message too. I didn't know who he was, but I knew it was a friend. After I had brought her son through, I told her that I had another male that wanted to step in. I received "Tony the Tiger" from the Frosted Flakes cereal as a symbol. This symbol was new to me, but Loved One's use things in my mind, so I knew it meant something.

I asked Tracey if knew someone named Tony, or if she had an affinity for Frosted Flakes cereal. She said no to the cereal but added that she knew two men named Antonio and that both had passed away. I told her I would ask for more evidence. When I did, I received the date December 12th. Tracey's eyes got big when I told her. She said that was day her ex-boyfriend Antonio had passed away. He provided more evidence and said he wanted to apologize sorry for things he had done in their relationship. Tracey was stunned because she received messages from her son and her ex-boyfriend. It was another piece of evidence to help Tracey know that our souls are still live on the Other Side.

Evelyn

Evelyn is a regular client. She loves to check in with her Loved Ones to see how they are. During a phone reading, her mom came through. Her mom shared the date of July 7th. I relayed this to Evelyn. She said she felt that her mom was suggesting a date for her wedding. At the time of the reading, Evelyn was in the midst of planning her wedding. July 7th was one of three days that she was considering for her wedding day.

After the reading, Evelyn said she was choosing July 7th for her wedding day. She also said that she would let me know how it went. I heard from Evelyn a few months later. She said that July 7th turned out to be a warning from her mom. Evelyn's daughter, Jazzy, had a seizure that day and had bleeding in her brain. Evelyn didn't get married that day but was lucky that she was there to take her daughter to the hospital for treatment.

Casey

Spirit had a Loved One who came through to share a name with a client named Casey. During the reading, Casey's grandmother stepped in. She provided some wonderful evidence to share with Casey, but Casey had been hoping to hear from another Loved One.

During the reading, my eyes went to the floor. The light of the sun through the blinds created a shadow of Benjamin Franklin's profile. I was a bit taken aback by this, but knew it was important. Normally, I will receive George Washington as a symbol if a message relates to money, but this was Benjamin Franklin. I informed Casey that I was being shown Benjamin Franklin, but I didn't know what it meant.

Casey gasped and told me that she had had a son named Benjamin. Benjamin passed unexpectedly of SIDS. Casey' grandmother shared that she was holding Benjamin and that he was fine. The grandmother wanted her to know that Benjamin was with her and that Casey didn't have to worry anymore. Casey was overwhelmed with joy. She told me that she had been beating herself up over her son's death. She was happy that her grandmother was taking care of him on the Other Side.

Helene

Spirit also brought Helene in to see me. Helene wanted to connect in with her husband who had committed suicide. His passing caused her to feel depressed and overwhelmed. As always, I didn't know any of this information before I read for her.

Her husband came through and told me what had happened. He said that she wasn't living life since his passing. He wanted her to release any guilt she felt and to start living life again. Then he told me that he wanted her to start dating again. I was told she would meet someone during the month of September. I shared this evidence with Helene. She validated that she had not been living. She also said that she didn't think that she could date again but was happy to hear that her husband had given his blessing. The reading provided Helene with a feeling of relief. She now knew that she could move on.

Fast forward to a year later. Helene contacted me and said that she had met a man in September and was now living with him. She was happy that she was able to let her husband go and start a new life with this man.

Code Words Given by the Loved One
Jill

During a few of my readings, I am given code words. A code word is a word given to me by the Loved One to share with the client, so they know the Loved one is there with them. When this happens, I am unaware that the code word was given until the client tells me about it. This was the case with Jill and her son.

Jill came to get a reading, and her son was listened in. As I read for Jill, a male stepped in. It turned out to be her husband. He shared that he passed of cancer. He gave more evidence and kept stressing a "red brick house." I relayed this evidence to Jill and asked her if they lived in a red brick house. She and her son immediately started crying. Jill admitted that she was skeptical of Mediums. Before the reading, she said that she would know her husband was really with her if he had me say the word "red." It turns out that Red was his nickname. After the reading Jill told me that she knew he was still with her and that the reading was real. She thanked me profusely and gave me a big hug.

Cheryl

I read for another client, Cheryl, via the phone. Her father came through in the reading. He gave me evidence about his life and passing, which Cheryl validated. She asked him questions and received the answers she needed. However, it wasn't until the end of the reading that Cheryl was 100% convinced it was him.

While I wrapped up the reading, I asked her dad if he wanted to share anything else. He said to share "goober peanut butter" and tell her that he loved her. I had no idea what goober peanut butter meant, but I knew it had to be important. I relayed the message to Chery. I told her that her dad was sending his love and that he said to tell you about "goober peanut butter." I asked her if that made any sense to her because no one had ever said that to me before. Cheryl immediately started laughing. She said that whenever her dad would say goodbye to her, he would always make the statement, "Goober and out." I was blown away when I heard this. Cheryl knew it was truly her father because he said goodbye in his special way.

Gwen

Spirit was instrumental when Gwen, a regular client, booked another reading with me. Gwen had seen me several times over the years when she got the feeling that she needed another reading. Gwen had been missing her sister and talked to her before coming to the reading. She had given her a code word to share with me. Gwen, of course, did not tell me this prior to the reading.

During the reading, Gwen's mother came through and gave her advice and evidence of what was happening in her daily life. Gwen asked if her sister was around, and I was able to bring her sister through. I told Gwen that her sister was here and was waiting for her mother to stop talking before she stepped in. As I started to connect in with Gwen's sister, she immediately said, "I love her dearly." I thought that this very generic and told Gwen this but I shared exactly what I heard. Tears rolled down Gwen's face. Gwen said that she had asked her sister to tell her that she "loved her." Gwen was overjoyed to hear this code word from her sister and knew that her sister was with her.

Loved Ones Sharing Things that They Saw
Theresa

Sometimes when I am giving readings, Loved Ones share information about things that have occurred since their passing. In other instances, they will share information about what is currently happening. This was the case for a client name Theresa, who I read for via the phone.

Theresa's grandmother came through and gave evidence, but Theresa had been hoping to hear from her daughter. Theresa's daughter came through and shared evidence of her unexpected passing. I shared this with Theresa, but she didn't believe it was her daughter.

I told Theresa exactly what was said, and she confirmed that this was true. Then her daughter told me that she could see her mom. She shared that her mom was currently sitting on her bed. I relayed this to Theresa, who started to cry hysterically. She validated that she was sitting on her daughter's bed. Theresa admitted that she wasn't sure what to expect from the reading before it started, but now knew without a doubt that her daughter was alive and with her.

Melissa

When Melissa came to see me for a reading, her mom immediately stepped in. Melissa had been missing her mom terribly because her mom had been the glue holding the family together. Her mom shared that Melissa was now stepping into that role. I relayed this evidence to Melissa, and the tears started rolling down her face. She said that it was all true.

Her mom then shared that Melissa "sees me looking back at her in a mirror." She kept telling me that it was in her bedroom. I shared this evidence with Melissa, stressing that she see her mom in her bedroom. Melissa started chuckling, and more tears rolled down her cheeks. She told me that she when she looked in her bedroom mirror, she could see her mom looking back at her.

Melissa said that she was looking at herself, but it wasn't her, it was her mom. After the reading Melissa was happy that her mom was with her to help her be the glue to mend the family after her passing.

Joanna

I had another interesting piece of evidence come through for my friend, Joanna. I had not seen Joanna in over six years, but when I saw a Facebook post about her mother's passing, I immediately called her to see how she was doing. Joanna had no idea that I was a Medium or that I had started a business. As we spoke, I realized that this call was a way for her mother to come through. I didn't know what to do, but I knew that Spirit was playing a role in this.

I decided that I had to tell Joanna that her mom was stepping in with me. So, I told her that I was a Medium and had started a business. I could tell that she was a bit skeptical but was open to having her mom give her a message. I shared with Joanna the evidence that I received from her mom. Joanna started to cry hysterically. I shared more evidence with her, which she validated. However, it was one piece of evidence that convinced Joanna that her mother was really coming through.

Joanna's mother told me about "licorice." I relayed this evidence to Joanna. She couldn't believe that I had said this. She told me that her mom's favorite candy was licorice, and she had recently bought some in her mom's honor. Joanna told me that she knew that this was real and that I had a gift. She was so thankful that I had called her.

Joanna also told me that she had been talking to her mom and asked for a sign that she was with her. That was when I called her out of the blue and gave her the message. Joanna said that I had given her a sign! She knew her mom was with her and felt blessed that I was able to give her a message.

Loved Ones We Don't Know Giving Messages
Allison

Many times, when giving readings a Loved One the client doesn't know or hasn't met comes through. I tell clients that they might know this Loved One, but the Loved One knows you and is coming through for a reason. This was the case with Allison, who had been referred to me by one of her friends.

Allison had never had a reading before and was excited to hear anything that I could tell her. Allison's great grandmother came through during the reading. Allison had never met her great grandmother but had heard stories of her from her family. Her grandmother and mother spoke about her all the time. I gave Allison some evidence that she was able to validate. She was, however, unaware of the next piece of evidence I shared.

Her great grandmother said that she didn't approve of Allison's mom's marriage to her father. I shared this with Allison, and she looked stunned. She hadn't known this but said that she would find out. Allison was grateful that her great grandmother came through and promised that she would let me know what she found out about her mom's marriage.

Allison contacted me a week later. She told me that she talked to her mother and confirmed that what her great grandmother had said was the truth! Allison found out that her great grandmother had been very fond of her mother and didn't want her to marry her father.

This was poignant because it spoke to a situation in Allison's life. Allison was going through a rough patch with her current boyfriend. She knew certain things had to change if she was going to commit to him. Her great grandmother wanted to help her fix this and to make sure that Allison's parents liked her boyfriend so that Allison wouldn't have to go through the same situation as her mother.

Wanda

Spirit also brought Wanda to me. Like many other, Wanda felt an "urge" to have a reading but wasn't sure why. She was drawn to my website. Wanda was into numerology (the study of numbers) and added up the address of my business. She felt that the sum was a sign from the Universe and booked a reading.

When I read for Wanda, I brought though her grandfather. Wanda knew a little bit about him from her family but had never met him. He shared that he loved dancing. I relayed this to Wanda. She just gave me a strange look and said that she had never heard of that. I continued to give her more evidence that she was able to validate. Then I closed the reading. She thanked me for her reading and left with a feeling of peace.

Wanda contacted me a few weeks. She had found out that her grandfather was a dancer! I was happy to receive this validation. She now felt that it was her grandfather who guided her to me. She was thankful and blessed because she felt that she now had a connection with him.

Kim

Kim was looking for validation on some recent information that she uncovered, and Spirit guided her to me. Recently, Kim discovered she had a half-brother and they were able to meet. She also found out that the man she thought was her real father was actually her stepfather.

When I read for her, her biological dad came through. He shared with me all the evidence that she had uncovered. Kim was overwhelmed that I had validated this information. She was happy to know that her read dad knew she existed and was currently in her life.

Loved Ones Telling the Client "Sorry..."

Often when I give reading, Loved Ones want to apologize to the person receiving the reading. You see, when we pass to the Other Side, we all go through a "life review." This is like seeing a movie of your life. During the review, you see everything you've done—the good, the bad, and the ugly—and how these actions have affected other people. The reason I receive many apologies from Loved Ones is because they want to make amends or ask for forgiveness. This was the case for my client, Matt.

Matt had heard about me from his daughter. He came to see me to get some guidance on things in his life, but Spirit had another reason in mind. When I read for Matt, his father stepped in with one "sorry" after another. I shared this with Matt, and his eyes became big. He told me that he couldn't believe that his father was coming to give him a message, but he was open to hearing what his father had to say.

Matt's father shared that he had not a nice man. He compared himself to "Hitler." I couldn't believe what I was hearing and asked him to repeat it a few times. He did, and I realized that I had heard correctly. I was reluctant to share this evidence with Matt. However, when something like this happens, I tell the client that the Loved One shared something that I normally would not say, and I ask them if they would like to hear what their Loved One relayed to me. I did this with Matt.

I told Matt that his father had not been a nice man. He agreed wholeheartedly. I asked Matt if he wanted me to share "verbatim" what I was being told. Matt said, "Tell me what he wants to say. I can take it." I then told him that his father compared himself to Hitler. Matt's eyes became big and he exclaimed, "YES! That is exactly who he was!" I was blown away and couldn't believe I was even sharing this evidence. I went on to share many more apologies from Matt's father that he wanted him to hear.

The father went on to share things that he did to Matt and his brother. I relayed this to Matt, and he validated the evidence. After the reading, Matt was overwhelmed and thanked me for helping him. He said knowing that his father was sorry would help him to finally begin healing his childhood wounds.

Peter

Peter's niece is a regular client of mine, but Spirit thought it was time that Peter came in to see me. I had recently given Peter's niece a message from her cousin. That cousin turned out to be Peter's son. As always, I didn't know this information before seeing Peter. I only knew she was bringing a man named Peter and that she wanted to be there for support.

Going into this reading, I knew Peter was skeptical because I could feel his energy. As I started to read, I asked him to just be open and let me bring in whatever it was that Spirit wanted him to hear. Immediate, I had a male that stepped in. I kept hearing the word "dad", but I didn't feel it was a dad. I was given the initial "B" and shared this evidence. Peter made a wailing sound. His son Ben had stepped in.

Ben shared that he had overdosed on drugs. He wanted to let his father know that he was alive. As I shared this evidence with Peter, he couldn't even look at me. Tears streamed down his face. Ben wanted his father to know that his passing was not his fault. He said he was sorry that he hadn't listened to his father. I found out that Peter did everything that he could to help his son, but he felt he didn't do enough. Ben wanted him to finally let this go. He told me that he could see how much pain his dad was in because of his actions.

After the reading, Peter gave me a big hug and told me that he was so grateful for this reading. He said that this reading made him believe in Mediums and knew that his son was still alive.

Kelly

A client called me to inquire about booking an appointment for one of her friends, Kelly. I was out of town giving readings in Las Vegas and I told the client I could give her friend a phone reading the following week. The client advised me the friend was feeling undecided about having a reading. That's when Teddy, my guide, told me to say the word "mom." I didn't understand what this meant but trusted in Spirit and relayed the message. My client gasped and said firmly, "She will call you soon."

Two weeks later the client booked a reading for her friend via Skype. When I started Kelly's reading, I immediately felt her sadness. First, her grandmother came through and gave her evidence. But I kept hearing someone say, "Mom, mom, mom." I told Kelly this. Tears rolled down her face as she realized it was her son, Scott.

Scott wanted to apologize to Kelly. He said me that he had overdosed on drugs and alcohol. His mother had warned him of the dangers, and he had had many opportunities to change his ways, but he didn't. Scott's addictions led to his passing. I relayed this to Kelly, and she validated the evidence.

Scott continued to say that he was sorry for all the pain he caused her and the rest of the family. He wanted her to know that he was doing just fine and was watching over all of them. After the reading, I noticed Kelly's demeanor change. She started to perk up. She was so happy to hear from her son and knew that he was alive on the Other Side. Kelly told me that she was grateful that she took a chance on the reading because she could now heal her broken heart.

Loved Ones Sharing Their Favorite Things
Amy

Loved Ones often talk about the things that they liked here while living on Earth. Many times, these favorite things can bring back wonderful memories and laughter to the client. This was the case with Amy, a returning client whose husband passed from cancer.

Amy was so distraught that her husband was gone that she was not living her life. During the reading, her husband provided wonderful evidence. He also made her laugh. Amy's husband told me about a jack in a box. No one ever used a jack in a box as a symbol before. I didn't know what it meant, but I shared the evidence with Amy. Amy and her family members started to hysterically laugh. Amy told me that Jack in the Box was his favorite fast food. He always wanted to eat there. Her husband was happy to finally see her laugh, and so was she.

Jennifer

Like Amy, Jennifer was distraught over the loss of a Loved One and was not living her life.

When I read for Jennifer, her son came through. He not only gave her evidence of his passing and favorite songs, he also told me to say, "Warm chocolate chip cookies." Sometimes I will get chocolate chip cookies, but this evidence was different because he kept stressing the word "warm." I relayed this evidence to Jennifer. She just grinned and shook her head with disbelief.

Jennifer told me that she and her son would go to a café and chat over "warm" chocolate chip cookies. He only liked warm chocolate chips cookies; he wouldn't eat them any other way. Her son said she should go and eat some warm chocolate chip cookies and that he would be right next to her. When I shared this with Jennifer, she just smiled, laughed, and tears rolled down her face. She told me that was his way of trying to cheer her up. When one of them was not feeling the best, they would go out for warm chocolate chip cookies to talk.

After the reading Jennifer thanked me for bringing her son through. She said that she knew he was with her and that she could now try to heal her heart.

Marcy

Marcy was referred to me by a friend. As I read for her, her mother stepped in to give a message. Marcy was a bit taken aback by this because she was not sure what to expect. Her mother shared evidence of her passing, but then started to tell me about birdhouses. I didn't know what this meant but relayed this evidence to Marcy. As soon as I told her this, tears started to run down her face. Marcy said that her mother loved to collect birdhouses.

After the reading, Marcy admitted that she had been a bit skeptical of Mediums but knew now that this it was real. She said that she knew her mother was there when she heard me say birdhouses. Marcy was grateful that I was able to connect in with her mother and that she was happy on the Other Side.

Marissa

Marissa is a client that I have done phone readings for over the years. Marissa loves receiving guidance from her father, to whom she was extremely close.

In one reading, her father stepped in to give his advice about her business. He said that she was working on selling her business and that she needed to stop worrying and celebrate instead. He kept saying, "celebrate and dance." Marissa laughed because her father's favorite song was "Celebration" by Kool and The Gang. Her father wanted her to know that her business would sell and that she should have fun. Marissa was happy to connect in with her dad and get his advice on her business.

Loved Ones that I Have Read on Earth and after Their Passing
Christina

One of the most interesting things that I have encountered is relaying a message from a Loved One that I read for during their time on Earth. This has happened a few times, and all I can say is that Spirit is amazing. I do want to note that even though I have given these clients readings, I was not aware of their deaths during their readings. I believe Spirit does this for a reason. This was the case for a client name Christina who found me on the Internet.

Christina came to see me to get guidance for the life that lay ahead of her. During the reading, I found that she had just overcome an addiction and was starting to become more spiritual. Christina had just turned 21. She had a bright future ahead of her.

After her reading, she asked if she could help at an upcoming event, I was hosting few weeks later. She said that she wanted to be around more spiritual people. I told her that I would love to have her, and we set up a time to meet. I gave her my business card, and she left with a few candles to burn. Two days before the event, I texted Christina to confirm all the details. She responded, saying that she would be there. The event came and went, and I never heard from her.

I thought this was odd but figured that maybe something came up. I tried contacting Christina a few times, but never heard back. I received a call from Christina's mother about a month later. Christina's mom had found my business card in Christina's purse. She told me that Christina had passed away early on the day of the event. Her grandmother had found her with the candles that she bought from me still lit. Christina's mother said that she didn't believe in Mediums, but she wanted to have a reading with me to see if I could bring Christina through. I advised her to take some time to grieve and then contact me when she was ready.

A few months had passed when from Christina's mother again. She booked a reading with me. During the reading, Christina immediately stepped in and said that she was doing fine. She gave me evidence that her heart had stopped from an accidental overdose, and her mother validated that evidence. Christina said that she had sent her mom a few coins. I relayed this evidence to her mother, and she laughed. She had just found two coins in her bedroom. They seemed to have come out of nowhere. Christina said that she was free of addiction and was finally happy. After the reading Christina's mother told me that she was now at peace. She knew that this was real, and that Christina was okay.

Jazzy

Earlier, I wrote about Evelyn, whose mother gave her the date July 7th. Initially, Evelyn thought her mom was providing a wedding date. Instead, it turned out to be warning. July 7th was the day Evelyn's daughter, Jazzy, had a seizure that resulted in a brain bleed.

I had done a phone reading with Jazzy three months before her seizure had occurred. At the time, Jazzy was 25 and working on her education. She had wanted a reading to get some guidance, but she also wanted to hear from her grandmother, whom she dearly missed. As I read for Jazzy, her grandmother shared some of their wonderful memories. She wanted Jazzy to keep up with her schoolwork and start to live life.

I saw both Jazzy and Evelyn a month before the seizure, so I was shocked when I had heard that Jazzy was in the hospital. She was on seizure medications, but the event took its toll. Two months after the brain bleed, Jazzy passed away. Evelyn shared this devastating news with me. She told me that when she was ready, she was going to have a reading with me. I told her to take her time to grieve her daughter's death and that I would be here to connect in with her daughter when she was ready.

I did a phone reading for Evelyn a few months later. Jazzy and Evelyn's mom immediately stepped in. Jazzy told me that she was with grandmother and that she was happy. Jazzy said she was finally free of the medications and that she was alive. I relayed this to Evelyn. I could hear her crying, but she said that she was so happy to hear from her daughter. Jazzy talked about her mom wearing her scrubs and that she needed to "pull up her pants." I shared this evidence with Evelyn, who laughed hysterically. She said that her scrub pants were falling off her, so she needed new ones. I gave Evelyn more evidence, which she was able to validate.

After the reading, Evelyn said that she was sad that Jazzy was no longer on Earth but was happy that she was with her parents. She knew that her daughter was doing just fine and was watching over her and that made her happy.

Steve

Spirit sent Steve to me through his daughter. The daughter was a regular client, but she wanted to book a reading for her dad. The daughter told me that Steve was sick and needed get in soon. Teddy, my guide, told me that I had to get him in. When I heard this, I knew that it was important. I told her that I would figure something out and get back to her. I finagled my schedule and read for her dad a few days later.

As soon as I started the reading, his father stepped in and gave evidence. However, it was his son that he wanted to hear from. His son stepped in after Steve's father and wanted to share that he was sorry that he hadn't listened to his dad. He said that he overdosed and now his dad was blaming himself. As I relayed this evidence to Steve, I heard him sobbing over the phone. Steve validated the evidence and told me that he was having a hard time in his life due to this. Steve's son provided more evidence, proving to Steve knew that it really was him. Steve thanked me profusely and told me that he could finally forgive himself. I told him that I was happy that to be the vessel and share him the message.

A few weeks later, Steve popped into my head. I kept thinking about him, but I couldn't figure out why. I found out a week later. A friend of Steve's daughter was taking my class and shared that Steve had passed due to cancer. I didn't realize that she knew Steve's daughter nor that he had cancer. Now I understood why Steve was on my mind. He was trying to give me a message. At that very moment, Steve stepped in because he wanted his daughter to know that he made it to the Other Side. He was with his son and that the reading allowed him to let go and not be fearful of dying. I shared this with my student so she could pass the message on to his daughter. After all this, I just shook my head because Spirit was instrumental in getting Steve to read with me so he could transition to the Other Side with ease.

COMMON QUESTIONS

I receive many questions from clients pertaining to my readings. Here are a few common questions that I receive which may help you too!

1. **"What the Difference is Between a Medium and a Psychic?"**

A Medium connects with Loved Ones that have passed and gives psychic information. However, a Psychic is **_not_** a Medium. A Psychic cannot connect to Loved Ones on the Other Side but can give psychic information. It is important to know the difference. If you want to connect in with a Loved One, you need to see a Medium.

2. **"Why Do Certain Loved Ones Come Through and Others Don't?"**

There are several reasons why this happens. Here are just a few reasons.

- The client is not ready to hear from the Loved One because there is so much grief involved.
- The client is not open to hearing the message from the Loved One.
- The Loved One may be busy on the Other Side. They have lives too, just like we do on Earth.
- The Loved One might be in a "cocoon stage." This means they are still healing on the Other Side.
- The Loved One that is stepping in may be coming to give an apology, or they might have gone through a similar situation and want to help.
- The Medium might not be the right person to connect to with the Loved One who the client wants to hear from.

I also want to add that some clients ask me if I can connect into a "certain Loved One." This just depends on the Loved One. When this happens, I ask my guide, Teddy, if I will be able to connect in with the Loved One at the time of the reading. Other times I have brought Loved Ones through if a client requests during the reading. However, this only happens if they are around, waiting and wanting to connect, but there is no guarantee the connection will happen. There have been times when the clients request for that particular Loved One comes in, and then other times when the Loved One does not.

3. "Is There Any Difference Between a Phone Reading and an In-Person Reading?"

There is no time or space with Spirit, and I am just the vessel. I do phone readings for people around the world. No matter how the reading is done via phone or in-person, I receive the same evidence from Loved Ones and relay it to the client.

4. "Do You Remember What You Told Me the Last Time I had a Reading?"

I am just a vessel, so I don't remember most people's readings. I have had several clients come back to me and I couldn't tell them what I said in previous readings. Nor could I tell them which Loved One had stepped in for them. The reason: I am just a messenger. If I remembered all this evidence, I would have libraries of information. It is not for me to remember the reading; it is for the client to remember the reading because the information is theirs alone.

5. "What is the Code Word or Name They Used for Their Loved One?"

Again, if it is something that the Loved One will share with me, I will pass it along. However, I am not going to hunt or search to receive the evidence. Hunting causes me to drop out of the link with the Loved One. When that happens, I am working psychically. It is also important to know that that some Loved Ones won't share the evidence with me. It just depends on the Loved One and if the evidence is in the dictionary of symbols that I use.

It is also important to note that when Loved Ones connect in with me clairaudiently, a different process is taking place. Most clients think that I hear dialog through my ears as if I am having a conversation. Unfortunately, that is not how I receive the evidence. I hear Loved Ones, through my mind. It is like a news ticker that runs at the bottom of the television screen. I am hearing words, but the words are not usually in complete sentences. If a Loved One is trying to give me a code word, it must be something in my dictionary. For example, if the code word is "gasket," I don't have a symbol for that. Instead, the Loved One may use the word "car."

FINAL THOUGHTS ON RECEIVING A READING

I often read for people who have never spoken to a Medium before. I wanted to share a few tips on receiving a reading.

1. **Don't be Nervous!** There is nothing to fear in a reading. Spirit has sent you to hear some evidence that you have been asking about! Just be aware: Sometimes the evidence is what you need to hear and not what you want to hear! This includes the Loved Ones that come through to give you a message.

2. **Have an Open Mind!** When you are having a reading, be open to the message and don't block your energy! Blocked energy means you are closed off to receiving evidence. When you block your energy, you are building a wall that I will have to tear down, and it will take time doing this. It makes sharing the message with you harder. You may miss out on more evidence that I could have provided. And you will have less time with the Loved Ones giving you their message.

3. **Are you Ready to Receive a Reading?** People often ask me to prove that I am a Medium. They want me to give them some information that only they would know before they book a reading. I see it this way: I don't need to prove anything to anyone. If you are ready to receive a reading from me, then your Loved Ones are "ready" to give me the evidence you need to hear! It is as simple as that!

AFTERWORD

Writing this book was a leap of faith for me. Over the past five years, Spirit and many other people have told me that I should write a book. My guide, Teddy, would tell me to "write." I would pick Oracle cards that spoke of writing. Or a student or client would say, "You do know that you should write?" I knew that I could write it, I just never really put too much effort into starting.

I finally gave in to Spirit and said, "Fine, I will start to write." I had no idea what Spirit wanted me to write about, but I've contemplated it over the years. I thought about writing self-help books or compiling my blogs into a book. I even worked on a children's book. Then I spoke to my friend, Jakki, who wrote the book *And That Day Came* a year ago. When I shared my ideas with her, she said it sounded like I should write a memoir. I had never thought of it that way. In late April 2019, I decided to share my story. I began writing my memoir, and this book emerged.

I now realize that Spirit knew this was the perfect time for me to start writing. As I replayed my life and wrote about my experiences, I was healing. Some of my stories brought me to tears while others filled me with complete joy. However, I realized, it was my relationship with mother that I really needed to heal from.

This book helped me see things from a different perspective. When I contemplated my childhood as an adult, I could step into my mother's shoes and understand why she did what she did. Allowing myself to be vulnerable as I wrote about my experiences helped me heal past pain and feel more love for my mother.

The Voice of Spirit urged me to write because they knew that my mother was going to pass. Writing each word of this book helped to prepare me for that loss. I am blessed that I had the opportunity to work on the leftover pieces I had not healed from. It was like I went back in time! I cleared and swept away the fragmented pieces that were associated with her. I was able to heal, without any regret, before her passing. I also had a different respect for her because I could understand how trapped she was in this world.

My mother had been follower, not a leader. This caused her to lose her way because she followed too many people down the wrong path. She didn't listen to her own voice or stand up for herself. I learned a lot from this. Seeing her unable to stand in her power taught me that I could, and should, stand in my own. I knew that I would not travel that same road as she did. This can be a hard realization, but it's important to know that people teach us lessons, both good and bad. My mother could not break the chains that bound her here on Earth, but I feel peace knowing that she is now free on the Other Side.

I realize now that my mother had had a complicated spiritual journey. She had been spiritual in the beginning of her life, lost it in somewhere in the middle because she didn't know how to use the energies or protect herself form them, but found it again at the end. As Nikki and I went through her things, I found many books, crystals, statues, etc. that were linked to spirituality. I felt in my heart that she tried to get back on the path but didn't have the strength. Her Earthly chains were just too strong.

Spirit has a way of showing you things that you couldn't see before. After her passing, I clearly saw that my mother had been an authentic, spiritual soul who became lost on her journey, and I commend her for trying to get back on the spiritual road. Now that she is on the Other Side, I will have a better relationship with her. I am looking forward to her helping me on the spiritual journey that lies ahead of me. I know that we will finally have mother-daughter relationship, and I do not take that for granted of what a blessing that is.

The other wonderful aspect of writing this book was reliving all the synchronicities that I experienced in my life. This was the first time I saw them all laid out in front of me. Seeing all of them together was amazing because I could clearly how Spirit had nudged me in certain aspects of my life. It was fascinating to see how one road lead to another and so on. I could see the links Spirit used to connect people, places, and things. I am so blessed that I was open to receiving these nudges and guidance from Spirit.

Lastly, I am truly blessed to be able to call myself a Medium. Using my abilities to help serve others brings happiness and joy to me. I have met so many wonderful clients and students who I have given guidance or healing to. I am blessed to be able to help steer them on their journeys ahead. Seeing people transform before your eyes is amazing. But watching them help others is a domino effect that I love being a part of. I know that none of this would have happened if I didn't walk down the spiritual path to accept my Mediumship abilities. My life would not be the same without the guidance from Spirit.

I am glad that I took that chance and walked down this spiritual road. It had not been an easy road, but it has made me stronger. I always say that everyone has a story, and this is mine. The strength, knowledge, and hard work that I endured now helps other. Not only have I healed, but I've helped others heal too. I am so honored and blessed to do this work. I will continue to push forward, to learn, to teach, and to grow. But most of all, I will continue to be **Guided by the Voice of Spirit**.

Chicks with Spiritual Gifts

For more information on Readings, Healings or Classes

Visit: Chickswithspiritualgifts.com

480-788-5540

Made in the USA
Lexington, KY
30 November 2019